ontents

In Appreciation. . .

Unexpressable gratitude and indebtedness to my parents, Alex and Marcia Rodriguez, for having had the courage and conviction to accept this gospel and then to teach me correct principles. Reciprocal feelings to Steve, laced with a devotion and respect that had its beginning in the eternities. A tender reverence to Steve for helping me to understand and live one of the Savior's greatest lessons, to turn the other cheek. . . .

SECOND EDITION

The publishers sincerely appreciate the overwhelming reception of *Self-Esteem for the Latter-day Saint Woman*. Particularly gratifying have been the many letters expressing thanks for the book's pertinent message. Sisters around the world have been aided in reaching their potential in joy and self-esteem. The publishers invite future letters from Anita's readers. In releasing this Second Edition, we hope to touch more lives and assist more sisters to enrich their self-esteem.

Self-Esteem for the Latter-day Saint Woman

Anita Canfield

Randall Book Company

ISBN No. 0-934126-15-1

First Printing, November 1980
Second Printing March 1981
Third Printing August 1981
Fourth Printing December 1981
Fifth Printing, December 1982
Sixth Printing, March 1983
Second Edition, November 1983

Randall Book Company
9500 South 500 West, Suite 103
Sandy, Utah 84070

Printed in the United States of America

Preface

There are so many books available that deal with values, ideals, goals, setting goals, how to raise good children, good husbands, good crops. There are books on sewing, canning, talents, love, marriage, neighbors, families, and relationships. This is a book about only you. It is meant to help you deal with all the pressures and guilt feelings those other books may create within you. This book is about yourself. More specifically, it is about your SELF ESTEEM.

Why is a book on self-esteem any different for a Latter-day Saint woman? Why is it important at all? Why should these words be directed specifically to the women of the Church?

Being a Latter-day Saint means you ascribe to a certain lifestyle and value system, a "uniform code" by which you live and grow. The code and the objective may be uniform, but the people aren't. You may belong to a group of women who uphold the same standards, goals, and beliefs, but you will find in this group the young and the old, the married and the single, the mother and the childless, the Indians and the chiefs, those who stay at home and those who work, the widowed, the divorced, those with inactive or non-member husbands, and those of other cultures, customs, and mores.

You women of the Church today are the most elect women on the earth because you are members of the Lord's true organization. You have to be strong women because you face daily opposition in a world growing with fears and doubts and disillusionment as Satan is working hard in his final hours. You have the highest goals and ideals of any women on earth. You *Want* to choose the right, and you dare to be different. You are strong because you have been saved to be born in this, the last dispensation of the gospel, and to be warriors for the Lord. Warriors need armor.

The battle is not at all easy, and Satan works overtime on you elect women.

This book is meant to be short and easy to read so that it can be read over and over again and in times of need. It is meant to be a "working lifetime investment plan." Your best investment is yourself. It has been written so that you can carry it with you in your purse to all those waiting places (at the doctor's, the dentist's, the bank, the hairdresser's, etc.). You can pick it up and work on any single facet for a few minutes every day. As soon as you finish reading this book, put it down for only one day, and begin reading it over again immediately.

This book is meant to *inspire* the reader to new levels of self-confidence, self-mastery, and self-esteem. Notice the word used was "inspire." This book won't develop those attributes; only you the reader can do that.

The chapters will center around the following five basic ideas and reasons self-esteem needs to be in focus in a specific way for Latter-day Saint women:

1. The principle of self-esteem is different for a woman in the Church from those not in the Church because she knows the concept and nature of God and has a clearer understanding of her origin, purpose, and goals in life. Satan works much harder and invests more time on such a woman because she does have such lofty goals. She also has such a tremendous influence on generations of lives in her family. Because of this concerted effort on Satan's part, she often succumbs to his words of discouragement and his innuendoes of personal weakness.

2. The LDS woman is encouraged to stay home in a day when the world around her is shouting "develop your identity." This causes frustration and guilt feelings. It also causes the LDS woman to feel inadequate around a non-LDS woman who is seemingly "expressing herself." The women of the Church need to grasp the concepts of self-fulfillment and self-development as suited to the Lord's ways and needs. They need to understand there is nothing wrong with their feelings — they are natural feelings. It is natural and Godlike to want to develop one's full potential and energies. A plan for priorities needs to be established to enable a woman to accomplish all she must do.

3. The LDS woman must assume the challenge and responsibility of being a lighthouse to the outside world which carefully observes her and will continue to do so even more in the future. The Latter-day Saint woman must not follow just any leader, but rather she needs to be prepared, as a lighthouse is prepared — as a beacon light to all the women in the world. She must understand with confidence her own views on morals, politics, religion, children, families. And as the world observes, she must look like a woman who does indeed have a personal relationship with God. That includes her personal appearance as well as the level of spirituality and confidence.

4. The power of the Priesthood is the greatest power on earth, and a woman can learn to benefit from that power and be a spiritual part of it. So many LDS women are threatened by the priesthood and don't understand their contribution to that power. The structure of the Church lends itself more to Priesthood dominated roles, and often the women of the Church feel they are given "second class" standings or considerations. This is largely due to how the women feel about themselves and not what is actually happening.

5. The LDS woman must be in command when seeking out and teaching the gospel to those with whom she associates. A woman with little self-esteem will not "seek out" others to teach

the gospel. With President McKay's decree "every member a missionary," came a challenge to the women of the Church. As the last hours roll forth, the great strength of the women in the Church can have a spiritual impact on the whole world if they have the self-confidence to "seek out" those who will hear the messages. In her family, in order for her to train up a generation of self-confident, self-mastered "warriors," she must respect and esteem herself. She must be a blessing to all those with whom she associates.

Everyone has feelings of discouragement and weakness. THAT IS OKAY. But these should be temporary feelings which are under the control and power of the person. If they are feelings that are ever present, personal progress stops.

This book is meant to inspire you to:

1. Think about yourself.
2. Be prayerful and ask Father in Heaven to help you gain control.
3. Be honest with yourself and help you determine your strengths and weaknesses.
4. Have only a positive attitude in knowing you will succeed.
5. Turn all your thoughts into ACTION.

Self-esteem is so fragile. It needs a gentle soil of identity in which to be planted, warmed by positive thoughts and actions, and fed by spiritual fruits and gifts. It can be trampled by thoughtless actions, or crushed by debilitating words, or withered by its own lack of spiritual nourishment. Each woman is her own gardener. She has within her the power to develop a good harvest and plant new generations of self-esteem and self-mastery. She has within her the power to become a greenhouse for new life and the source of survival for others. She has within her the power to sublimate all of her natural inborn tendencies and attributes into Godhood.

Chapter  One

Identify Yourself

Let's begin with a simple exercise.

How would you describe a person without any reference to her talents, knowledge, looks, or accomplishments? Stop here and consider someone you know; think carefully about that statement and then describe that person.

This would have been impossible for you to do unless you knew that individual personally. You could not describe a person with any degree of depth unless you were well acquainted with that person. How many times have you misjudged someone's character or personality simply by taking into consideration only their external appearances. After spending time getting better acquainted with them, don't you often discover they are quite different from that first impression?

Let me describe a friend of mine to you.

She has a wonderful sense of humor which puts any person immediately at ease. This friend looks you straight in the eye, never gazing away. There is a genuine concern there for others' needs. She demonstrates compassion and care, is thoughtful, considerate, and takes great effort in discovering what special gifts she can give others to delight them. This wonderful woman is unselfish and would give you whatever she had that she thought you might need. She cares for her ailing mother and encourages her constantly. My friend has a serious illness that causes her great pain, yet she never complains. She is happy, friendly, and has great courage and common sense.

Now you have no idea what she looks like, what her knowledge is, what talents she may have, or if she has accomplished much at all in her life. But you already know her. This description has influenced you to think of her in a positive way. It makes no difference that she is a tiny, five-foot blonde, slightly overweight, has a high school education, is an accomplished equestrian, plays the piano, is an entrepreneur in real estate, has a husband and three sons, and is not a member of the Church. Would your opinion of her be different had you only known the "physical facts" about her first?

We have not seen the Savior, and yet when we describe Him, we describe qualities. The more qualities we discover about Him, the better we have come to know Him.

Describe yourself without any reference to your talents, knowledge, looks, or accomplishments. This would be impossible for you to do unless you really know yourself, unless you are honest with yourself, and have spent time in getting acquainted with You.

Getting to know yourself requires total honesty on your part. Shakespeare put it poetically: "This above all, to thine own self be true and it must follow, as the night the day — thou canst not then be false to any man."

This is an important constructive step to a healthy self-esteem. You must be honest enough with yourself to describe who you are without any reference to your looks, talents, knowledge, or accomplishments. You must be honest enough with yourself to acknowledge your qualities and strengths, as well as your weaknesses and flaws in character. You must be willing to study and search out WHO YOU ARE. It does require *study*. It also takes a great deal of courage to admit what it is you like and don't like about yourself. *Honesty with self is getting control over emotions; it is getting in touch with feelings; it is identifying cause and reaction.*

For example, when I was in college, there was a tall, statuesque beauty who dressed like a Paris model. I never liked her. I found fault with her constantly, until one day I got in touch with my feelings. "Anita, you are jealous of her." I made myself admit that. It's something you really know deep down inside, but the conscious mind just lets it pass by. Once I had made that painful observation, it was easy for me to control the emotions, find her qualities, learn from her, and thus, overcome jealousy.

On a lighter side, once I thought it was important to be considered "socially" fashionable. Since tennis was the current fashionable and chic sport, I went out and bought balls, shoes, racket, darling outfit, and lessons. All through the lessons, I kept thinking about everything but tennis (mostly the instructor — he was gorgeous). Every day I practiced, took lessons, practiced, took more lessons, practiced harder. I would get up at 7:00 a.m. to practice because it was so hot later in the day. It was so boring hitting that ball back and forth against the board. Perspiration poured down my face; I hated it. Things just weren't coming together. One morning as I was hitting that ball, bored to death, I stopped, looked at the whole situation, and admitted to myself, "Anita, you don't even like this; what are you doing here?" I decided that to be honest was better than to be chic. I walked off the court, handed my racket and balls to some kids, and have never been back. It had been dishonesty with myself that kept me there and wasted time I could have used in other interests. (I also learned a great appreciation for tennis players; they have *real* talent and self-discipline!)

When I begin to have illusions of grandeur, or delude myself with rationalization, or start becoming negatively oriented, I try to whisper, "Now, Anita, you're just not going to get away with that." It works. In the winter I try to run almost every day. In the summer, I use an indoor trampoline. With a heavy stress schedule, my physical metabolism depends upon this vigorous activity. After several days of sleeping in, one morning I said, "Okay, one more morning to sleep in, I don't need to run today." Then I heard that little voice, "Anita, you're just not going to get away with that." I heard it one day when I thought I had justification for being angry at a subcontractor. I've heard it more than once when I thought my family was too demanding on me. I've heard it when I wanted to avoid an assignment or an unpleasant duty. It's a haunting little voice, but once you get used to it, it becomes an asset to being honest with yourself. Try it next time you are tempted to rationalize anything.

The *first* goal to honesty with self is to get in touch with your feelings. Be honest with yourself about what you like and don't like, about what you can and can't do, about why you do or don't do certain things, such as, "I really don't like playing tennis," "I am jealous," "I did it because I wanted them to think I was neat."

The *second* goal to honesty with self is not to feel guilty for feeling the way you do. If it is a negative response or attribute, then you can begin to correct the flaw, such as jealousy, pride, etc. If it's simply a matter of not being of your nature (for example, tennis or changing diapers or sewing), don't inflict guilt feelings. It's okay if you don't like things that are seemingly important, fashionable, or the ideal.

The *third* goal is to recognize what is or is not a character flaw, and then go about rectifying it.

The *fourth* goal to honesty with self is to be honest with others about yourself. Don't try to cover your weaknesses with lies such as, "I can't do it because I have a sore throat." When it should be, "I can't do it because I simply haven't planned for it. I forgot to allow enough time." We had a family home evening in which we discussed this open honesty of admitting when we were wrong. We found that as a family, there were many times during a day we weren't honest with each other — the "it's-not-my-fault" syndrome. Being able to apologize falls under this category. It's a great way to practice honesty with self.

Being honest with yourself and others about your feelings produces these benefits:

1. *You are able to distinguish quality from weakness.* As you admit what you like and don't like about yourself, logically you will determine what is strength — that which motivates you — and what is weakness — that which holds you back.

2. *You are able to instigate change or improvement.* As you determine weakness versus strength, you will have greater powers over your mind because (1) you have had the courage to be honest and (2) you have the desire to improve — or you wouldn't have found it necessary for honesty.

3. *You gain greater insight not only in your personal life but also in the lives of husband, children, friends, family.* It helps you see what makes *them* "tick." You are able to analyze what they are doing and why. Once you have understood your own motives and actions, it is easier to understand why others do and say the things they do. You have a point of reference.

4. *Your personality develops because of honesty when you aren't overridden with guilt feelings.* Honesty relieves guilt feelings because you don't have to "fight" any false ideas or "struggle" with rationalizing weak behavior. You can attack the problem head-on. You are *mentally* free to develop your personality further by (1) concentrating on strengths and taking advantage of strong points and (2) setting goals to overcome weakness.

5. *You gain greater confidence and self-esteem; you don't have to pretend a part or role.* You and others know what makes *you* "tick." Your honesty enables you to feel confident in *who* you are and appreciate your personal qualities. You and others know you aren't concerned about being compared to anyone except your own physical progress. You and others know what your own personal objectives are — those that will cause you to rise to Godhood.

As a Latter-day Saint, you are told that:

You are a daughter of God.

You lived with Him before you came to this earth life.

He loves you dearly.

It is possible to become like God.

These statements are common and generally-known information by the members of the Church, probably appearing in many patriarchal blessings. Upon closer examination and thoughtful consideration of those phrases, therein lie the keys and secrets to who you really are.

1. YOU ARE A DAUGHTER OF GOD

You are a literal daughter of a literal God, an offspring of *The God.* You are worth a great deal just because you exist. We note how children in mortal life resemble their parents in feature, stature, and often personality traits. Therefore, if you are God's daughter, you must resemble Him, at least in the quality of His character. He made man in His image.

> And I, God, said unto mine Only Begotten, which was with me from the beginning: Let us make man in our image, after our likeness; and it was so. And I, God, said: Let them have dominion over the fishes of the sea, and over the fowl of the air, and over the cattle, and over all the earth, and over every creeping thing that creepeth upon the earth.

> And I, God, created man in mine own image, in the image of mine Only Begotten created I him; male and female created I them.

> And I, God, blessed them, and said unto them: Be fruitful, and multiply, and replenish the earth, and subdue it, and have dominion over the fish of the sea, and over the fowl of the air, and over every living thing that moveth upon the earth. (Moses 2:26-28)

Notice that God gave man *dominion* over "all the earth." Man (meaning male and female) is the superior intelligence on the earth. Already in the order of all things, you can see yourself placed far above any other level of life.

"For thou hast made him a little lower than the angels, and hast crowned him with glory and honour." (Psalms 8:5) This illustrates that as glorious as the angels of Heaven are, man is placed only "a little lower."

Man is God in embryo. Parley P. Pratt, in *Key to Theology,* says:

> An intelligent being, in the image of God, possesses every organ, attribute, sense, sympathy, affection that is possessed by God himself. But these are possessed by man, in his rudimental state, . . .these attributes are in embryo; and are to be gradually developed. They resemble a bud, a germ, which gradually develops into bloom, and then, by progress, produces the mature fruit, after its own kind. (pp. 100-101)

It is interesting to note here, too, that he closes that statement saying, ". . .by progress, produces the mature fruit, after its own kind." By *progressions,* you are what you make of yourself. Humans have a habit of saying when one is groping around in life, that she hasn't "found" herself yet. This statement is totally false. Self is not found; self is created.

It is overwhelming to ponder the thought that a Man who could create such an earth, such beings, such beauty, wealth, vastness, and splendor, REALLY IS OUR FATHER.

Some time ago, three women were having dinner. One was

7

LDS, one was Jewish, and one was Catholic. The Jewish woman had recently returned from touring a local LDS temple grounds and posed several questions about Mormon life. Then the Catholic woman asked a few more questions. Before long, they were all deep in conversation about the Church, especially the identity of God. As they talked on, it was explained how the Church goals are in line with the principle, "As man now is, God once was; as God now is, man may become." Having been taught to fear God as a Being they did not relate to, the non-LDS women felt it was a sin to consider man in the same sentence with God. They felt they would be bringing God down to man's level. Had they understood *who* they really were, they could have maintained a different relationship with God. Thus, they would have seen the great concept of not bringing God down to man's level, but rather, bringing man up to God's level!

How can you not consider yourself (as Parley P. Pratt described) graceful, intelligent, elegant, of great worth, when realizing the heritage that is yours? The world raves of its great lines and descendants of kings, queens, pioneers, pilgrims, statesmen, celebrities; families boast of ties and relations that have been renowned and recognized world-wide, nationwide, even locally. An older gentleman once introduced himself and then his wife, and in the same breath, mentioned that his son-in-law was so and so who had appeared in an academy award winning film.

Even among the members of the Church, we are proud to look back on heritage and whether or not a Smith, a Young, a Snow, etc., appears in our genealogy.

This same identification and esteem should be recognized and felt when we consider and ponder that we have such a great heritage. We are daughters of God, handmaidens of the Lord.

Wordsworth, a great mind and poet, pondered life and its miracles. He must have been inspired as he wrote:

Our birth is but a sleep and a forgetting;
The soul that rises with us, our life's star,
Hath had elsewhere its setting
And cometh from afar;
Not in entire forgetfulness,
And not in utter nakedness,
But trailing clouds of glory do we come
From God, who is our home.

2. YOU LIVED WITH HIM BEFORE YOU CAME TO EARTH

That tells you that you had a good relationship with your Father. You sat at His feet for instruction and love. You lived *with* Him. Living with a God and receiving instruction, you learned many things. It has been thought that all that has been written, said, composed, invented, or thought in mortality is only "re-remembering" what was once known in pre-earth life, what was taught to you there. You were given and taught certain gifts and talents that would be of value to you on earth. Coming to mortality, the veil was drawn, but the gifts and talents remain. Some are more apparent; others need discovery or cultivation.

> The pre-existent life was thus a period — undoubtedly an infinitely long one — of probation, progression, and schooling. The spirit hosts were taught and given experiences in various administrative capacities. Some so exercised their agency and so conformed to law as to become 'noble and great'; these were foreordained before their mortal births to perform great missions for the Lord in this life. . .Mortal progression and testing is a continuation of what began in pre-existence. (McConkie, *Mormon Doctrine*, p. 590)

Do you believe you were among those who thus lived so nobly? Believe it.

> *My sheep hear my voice*, and I know them, *and they follow me.* (John 10:27)

> All men do not come into this world with the same inclination toward or receptiveness of spiritual things. One of the greatest

endowments a mortal man can receive is the gift of spirituality, the talent and ability to recognize and cleave unto the truth. 'My sheep hear my voice, and I know them, and they follow me,' our Lord said. That is, his sheep so lived in pre-existence as to develop the gift of spirituality there; then coming to mortality, they brought that talent with them, and consequently they find it easy to believe and follow the true Shepherd. (McConkie, *Mormon Doctrine*, p. 761)

Remember that the Lord said all things to Him are spiritual. "All things unto me are spiritual, and not at any time have I given unto you a law which was temporal. . ." (D & C 29:34) This includes all your gifts and talents.

You heard His voice, and you recognized it; you are a member of His Church. And if mortal life is but a continuation of what you began in the pre-existence, what did you begin there, what did you learn? Certainly, as one of the "noble and great" you were given great talents and abilities.

Sometimes mortal life is only a re-remembering.

There was a young woman, 28 years old, with a severe handicap that prevented her from freely communicating with those around her. When she spoke, she uttered ugly, raspy, shrill noises that were more like squawks than words, and she was totally incomprehensible. She wasn't of a feeble mind; as a matter of fact, she was very intelligent. Her handicap prevented the words from forming. She wrote (in her own words):

> *In college I wanted to play tennis so badly. I was treated or ignored badly by the better players, and up went a mental block to learning. The frustration and tears!*
>
> *But as I got closer to Heavenly Father, He helped move the block.*
>
> *This lady I've played with is surprised at my improvements!*

I believe I already knew how to play! It was a spiritually created talent. This experience is very special to me because of all the trials I've suffered for it. The frustration has been a heavy amount.

And there were other talents with which she did the same.

The self-esteem on this young woman's face was so apparent as she interacted with others. No one could defeat her now. She had gained self-respect and self-esteem through "re-remembering" her talents of a former life. And she knew it. Yes, she had suffered, *but* she was willing to *pay the price.* The Lord gives us much but expects much also. She could not have gained as much self-esteem had she not drawn near to Him and realized her former life and worth. And where would she be had she not?

A noted surgeon, commenting on the athletes of the Olympic Games, said that humans have an enormous capacity for strength and ability, physical and mental, and at present, we have only tapped two to eight percent of it.

What would happen if we tapped more? What would we accomplish if we used even 25 percent of our ability? Man "possesses every organ, attribute, sense, sympathy, affection that is possessed by God Himself." Think how much we could progress towards Godhood.

Try to tap more. Discover about yourself what you already really know. Re-learn your former created talents. And then re-learn more.

A friend once said she had practiced long hours in preparation for her next piano lesson. She wanted perfection. Her small baby, household duties, and interruptions in her daily routine made it not at all easy. When the lesson was over, it wasn't what she'd wanted. She knew it, and the instructor knew it, and he said, "It wasn't what you wanted." She cried copious tears. How did he know the hours she had sacrificed to practice, worthy hours? But he said, "You haven't yet paid the price for the results you want." And he was right.

It was a high caliber and quality of training you were going through in the pre-existence, and so, desiring this level of excellence has made it easier to embrace and recognize the gospel in mortal life. What price are you willing to pay to keep that level of excellence?

It is exciting to consider the people who sat together and talked and shared love and counsel at these "Schools in Heaven." We clamor to the television set at conference time to be instructed by the prophet. Would you long to be in a room and instructed by Mozart or Bach if your love is music? If art is your nature, would you desire a friendship with Michaelangelo or Renoir or Ruebens? Consider long chats with Shakespeare, Keats, or Longfellow. Would deep friendships with such as these inspire or elevate you? Would you have more self-esteem because of their friendship and love for you? Would you feel a surge for excellence? Would you feel you were a better person for knowing them? Would they help elevate your opinion of yourself?

Now consider yourself as you were, a spirit child desiring good and excellence for yourself. Your friends and companions there were of those who wanted the same things. They were of the same mind, caliber, and training. Where are they now to inspire, to lift and elevate you? All around; look in your stake, in your ward, in your neighborhood, in your very home. These are they who shared with you counsels and talents. These are they who also desired to give the Lord a willing heart and mind, who were instructed and trained, and who have recognized Him here in mortal life.

Do not be threatened that Sister Stake Music Leader can play the piano better than you, or that Sister Bertha Breadmaker, who can make the greatest bread ever, has put you in charge of bread-making for Relief Society, or that Sister Sleek and Chic, who always looks like she stepped off the cover of a magazine, has asked you to be the Beautification Chairman, or that Sister

Smoothtalker has a wonderful way with words and vocabulary and they just made the two of you visiting teaching companions. If these sisters have achieved a level of excellence in a certain area, it's because they have *paid the price.*

Put earth aside. Remember you were together in those councils in Heaven. And there was a rapport and comraderie there that endeared us one to another. Remember that the Church is still school. We are here to learn and help each other (and that means you also help those who need your help and your talents). If there are those with talents and qualities that you admire but lack yourself, learn to:

1. Accept that fact.
2. Be inspired by that person.
3. Ask for their help in that area ("seek ye diligently and teach one another. . ." D & C 88:118).
4. Practice those talents or qualities that you desire. Don't say you can't do something or that you have no talents, but rather, you're having a little harder time "remembering"!

3. HE LOVES YOU DEARLY

Sometimes our sins are sins of commission and sometimes sins of omission. We suffer and we think, "How could God love me?" These are negative and critical thoughts. Have you ever said the following statements to yourself: "I feel worthless." "No matter how hard I try to be perfect, the more I realize how weak I am." "I fail at everything I try." "I feel out of place at church. Everyone there but me seems to have her life in order."?

There was Nephi, a great prophet of the *Book of Mormon.* Here was a strong man in body, mind, and spirit. Did his self-esteem ever suffer? Did he ever have negative thoughts? Was he ever discouraged?

Yes to all of those. Hated by his brothers, almost thrown into the sea, his life threatened again and again, he suffered constant harassment and scorn by his people, yet he took encouragement in the fact that he knew God loved him:

> Behold, my soul delighteth in the things of the Lord; and my heart pondereth continually upon the things which I have seen and heard.

> Nevertheless, notwithstanding the great goodness of the Lord, in showing me his great and marvelous works, my heart exclaimeth: O wretched man that I am! Yea, my heart sorroweth because of my flesh; my soul grieveth because of mine iniquities.

> I am encompassed about, because of the temptations and the sins which do so easily beset me.

> And when I desire to rejoice, my heart groaneth because of my sins; nevertheless, I know in whom I have trusted.

> My God hath been my support; he hath led me through mine afflictions in the wilderness; and he hath preserved me upon the waters of the great deep.

> He hath filled me with his love, even unto the consuming of my flesh.

> He hath confounded mine enemies, unto the causing of them to quake before me.

> Behold, he hath heard my cry by day, and he hath given me knowledge by visions in the nighttime.

> And by day have I waxed bold in mighty prayer before him; yea, my voice have I sent up on high; and angels came down and ministered unto me.

> And upon the wings of his Spirit hath my body been carried away upon exceeding high mountains. And mine eyes have beheld great things, yea, even too great for man; therefore I was bidden that I should not write them.

> O then, if I have seen so great things, if the Lord in his condescension unto the children of men hath visited men in so much mercy, why should my heart weep and my soul linger in the valley of sorrow, and my flesh waste away, and my strength slacken, because of mine afflictions?

> And why should I yield to sin, because of my flesh? Yea, why should I give way to temptations, that the evil one have place in my

heart to destroy my peace and afflict my soul? Why am I angry because of mine enemy?

Awake, my soul! No longer droop in sin. Rejoice, O my heart, and give place no more for the enemy of my soul.

Do not anger again because of mine enemies. Do not slacken my strength because of mine afflictions.

Rejoice, O my heart, and cry unto the Lord, and say: O Lord, I will praise thee forever; yea, my soul will rejoice in thee, my God, and the rock of my salvation.

O Lord, wilt thou redeem my soul? Wilt thou deliver me out of the hands of mine enemies? Wilt thou make me that I may shake at the appearance of sin?

May the gates of hell be shut continually before me, because that my heart is broken and my spirit is contrite! O Lord, wilt thou not shut the gates of thy righteousness before me, that I may walk in the path of the low valley, that I may be strict in the plain road!

O Lord, wilt thou encircle me around in the robe of thy righteousness! O Lord, wilt thou make a way for mine escape before mine enemies! Wilt thou make my path straight before me! Wilt thou not place a stumbling block in my way — but that thou wouldst clear my way before me, and hedge not up my way, but the ways of mine enemy.

O Lord, I have trusted in thee, and I will trust in thee forever. I will not put my trust in the arm of flesh; for I know that cursed is he that putteth his trust in the arm of flesh. Yea, cursed is he that putteth his trust in man or maketh flesh his arm.

Yea, I know that God will give liberally to him that asketh. Yea, my God will give me, if I ask not amiss; therefore I will lift up my voice unto thee; yea, I will cry unto thee, my God, the rock of my righteousness. Behold, my voice shall forever ascend up unto thee, my rock and mine everlasting God. Amen. (2 Nephi 4:16-35)

Read and re-read this psalm. You can almost hear the voice of this great man, to whom the Lord has shown great things, "yea; even too great for man. . ." It is so tender to realize he had the same feelings of frustration and weakness as we do. But he knew what it was to have himself encircled in the Lord's love and what self-esteem that brings!

Negative thoughts and discouragement are Satan's tools, not the Lord's.

Yes, you must be conscious of your weaknesses and failings, and repent of them. But it is Satan who causes you to dwell on them and leaves you feeling weaker and weaker and doubting your self-worth. The Lord wants to strengthen you and give you power to overcome your weaknesses:

> And if men come unto me I will show unto them their weakness. I give unto men weakness that they may be humble; and my grace is sufficient for all men that humble themselves before me; for if they humble themselves before me, and have faith in me, then will I make weak things become strong unto them.

President Lorenzo Snow said:

> And if we could read in detail the life of Abraham, or the lives of other great and holy men, we would doubtless find that their efforts to be righteous were not always crowned with success. Hence we should not be discouraged if we should be overcome in a weak moment; but, on the contrary, straightway repent of the error or the wrong we may have committed, and as possible repair it, and then seek to God for renewed strength to go on and do better. (Snow, "Blessings of the Gospel," *Ensign*, October 1971, p. 19)

Emerson said, "A man is what he thinks about all day long." And the great philosopher, Emperor of the Roman Empire, Marcus Aurelius, put it this way: "Our life is what our thoughts make it." It was Isaiah that said it the best, "As a man thinketh so is he."

If you think happy thoughts, you will be happy. If you think fearful thoughts, you will be fearful. If you think sickly thoughts, you will be ill. If you think failure, you will fail. If you wallow in self-pity, no one will want to be near you.

No one really knows how far the mind can actually go in influencing our lives. Certainly it changes outward physical appearance (facial expressions, posture, weight control, grooming). It can produce great spirituality within us, and it can delineate our personal qualities to any height or depth. It can carry a soul to the point of desperation or insanity, or to the heights of accomplishment and achievement. All these are possible, depending on what and how we think.

Years ago, the famous psychologist, William James, labeled his "as if" concept. He said that we cannot instantly change our *emotions* just by telling ourselves in the mind to do so, but that we can instantly change our actions. When we change our actions, we will automatically change our emotions (or feelings).

He said, "The sovereign voluntary path to cheerfulness, if your cheerfulness be lost, is to sit up cheerfully and to act and speak *as if* cheerfulness were already there."

Does it sound too simple? It is just that — simple! This is a POWER, the power of the mind to control the matter. It is a real POWER, like any other POWER such as walking through walls or healing the sick. It is a power that God has given to man to defend himself against Satan. "And I will put enmity between thee and the woman, between thy seed and her seed; and he shall bruise thy head, and thou shalt bruise his heel." (Moses 4:21)

The Lord said Satan would have power over mankind, ("bruise his heel") but that man would have greater power over Satan ("bruise his head"). It is through the POWER of the mind this is done. How else does Satan have power over us, except through our thoughts? Every action is precipitated by a thought. We thwart Satan by our thoughts — no other way.

There is an elderly woman I know. She is in every description an old woman. If she would only apply this principle, she could banish all her troubles within 24 hours.

She's in her eighties and a widow. She has yet useful things to do, council to give, and love to share. But does she try? No. She complains and whines of her problems and troubles. She almost reproaches you for being happy in her presence. She complains of her family being stingy and selfish — that no one brings her gifts, and if they do, they are not expensive enough. She dwells on her past youth, and is extremely vain about her age, telling no one the truth and pretending she is much younger. She scathes and berates her family in front of each other. Now they avoid her, trying to maintain some affection of the heart towards her.

The tragedy of the situation is that she could change herself from an unhappy, bitter, miserable, "old" woman into a loving and beloved grandmother, an honor unto her family. If she *wanted* to do it, all she would have to do is act happy, act unselfish, act as if she had love to give away, and it all would happen.

My own little grandmother, Mamagrande, is such a woman, honored and beloved by her family. Even the smallest children sense there is something regal and special about this tiny pint sized lady. There is not one vain bone in her, and she is truly without guile. All those who meet her instantly fall in love with her. She is so precious to all of us. Life gave her lemons, and she made lemonade.

Rafaela Garcia, at age thirteen, came to the United States with her mother and sister from Mexico after her father had been killed in the revolution. They came by mule over the mountains with no money and no personal belongings of any significance. They arrived in Texas, speaking no English. An uncle met them and helped them for a while.

Mostly because she knew her duty was to make her own way and to relieve the strain of "mouths to feed," she married my grandfather when she was sixteen.

During her married life, she lived most of it in extreme poverty. All of her children were born at home without help, not even the help of her husband. For a time, she was a "servant" to her husband's family, as was the custom. She spent two years of her life living (with four babies) in a filthy border town where "the flies on the meat at the market made it look black." She reared her seven children in a two-room shack by the railroad tracks, with no indoor plumbing, sinks or toilets, and an old coal-burning stove to heat the home and cook the food. My grandfather was a carpenter for the railroad and made $25.00 a month. They got their fresh vegetables by running after the produce trucks as they made their way to the Commission Road markets. The children gathered up whatever spilled off the back. They took turns buying clothes and shoes. If one needed new shoes and it wasn't his or her turn, they simply went without. One quart of milk was all they could afford for seven children for the whole week. Mamagrande had no education. She was not a member of the Church, but she believed that God would help her raise her children. She reared those children and taught them to believe in themselves. She could have said, "Well, life has given me lemons; there's nothing I can do about it. This is our lot in life. We live in the worst slums in Houston; there is nothing we can do. We haven't got a chance."

But she made lemonade. She taught her children self-reliance, the attitude of positive thinking, and that they must be the *best* they can be. She taught them without any personal education, but by her example. Never complaining, never seeing the mud, only the stars, always being positive, she taught with impact. Out of those seven slum children, here are their accomplishments:

Son — Retired Army Officer

Son — Pharmacist and successful businessman, self-employed

Son — Chemical engineer, designed Gulf Corporation oil refinery

Son — Graduated Stanford University, engineer and scientist, helped plot course to moon (my father)

Daughter — Real estate tycoon, worth several million dollars, Spanish scholar and linguist

Daughter — Artist and instructor, married to a banker

Son — Obstetrician-gynecologist-investor-millionaire

Life gave her lemons, and she gave it back lemonade.

My father told me that when he was 19 years old, he went to war from that slum home. When he returned, after having exposure to the world, he only then realized how sad the living conditions were and helped his parents get out of there. But what he said revealed the mighty force of positive thinking to me: "Anita, we were poor, and we didn't even know it!"

I love Mamagrande for that. Today, in her humble way, she says she doesn't think she's done anything notable in her life. If you were to see her on the street, you would probably walk right by, seeing nothing more than a pint-sized, white-haired old woman with twisted, calloused hands. She never read Emerson's essay on self-reliance; she may not even know who he is. But she changed the course of generations of lives by her positive mental attitude. The list of accomplishments of her grandchildren and great grandchildren (numbering over 100) would fill a book alone. If you ask her what advice she has for a good life, she will say:

> *"Love God and thank Him.*
> *Just be happy every day.*
> *Work hard and do your best."*

How long would it take you to succeed if all you did was surround yourself with thoughts of failure, thinking failure, dressing like a failure, and always complaining? You would never succeed.

Yet thousands of women do this every day. In their daily work, Church work, their lives in general, they seem satisfied with spiritual or material poverty. They have ceased any real effort to rise out of it. Look around you; look in your own mirror. What reflections do you see? Is there NO EXPRESSION? I see so many expressionless faces. They seem to be saying, "I can't. This is my lot in life. Here is where I'll stay."

It is not your lot in life; you possess every organ and attribute that is possessed by God himself. Within you lies POWER — the

POWER of positive thinking. It is faith. Faith sufficient to produce the power. If you allow the doubts to creep into your thoughts (and they will), and if you do not thrust them out, you will doubt everything that is in your path. All your stepping stones will become your stumbling blocks.

I got my patriarchal blessing when I was nine years old. My parents had been converts to the Church for a little over one year. The gospel was the illumination of our home, and it was centermost in my nine-year-old thoughts. I wanted that blessing for my birthday. As we were leaving his home that day, the patriarch leaned over and said, "Anita, live each day as though it was your last day on the earth." In my young mind, I didn't completely understand what he meant. As the years went by, I thought he had counseled to avoid sin. But now I know he meant what the Savior meant when he said: "Take therefore no thought for the morrow, for the morrow shall take thought for the things of itself. Sufficient is the day unto the evil thereof." (3 Nephi 14:34)

Realizing that in Jesus' day the word "thought" meant "anxiety," what the Lord was saying is don't *worry* about tomorrow, concern yourself only with today. There is enough evil in one day to contend with in that time frame.

Doubts, fears, lack of faith, worry about the things unseen or undone all add up to negative thinking. If a woman's mind is grayed by any of those, how can she achieve?

Thomas Carlyle said, "Our main business is not to see what lies dimly in the distance, but to *do* what lies clearly at hand."

Positive mental attitude is believing in yourself and what you can do. It is taking positive steps toward accomplishment. It is not running faster than you have strength. (See D & C 10:4.) It is not letting the difficulties overwhelm or discourage you. Someone once said, "I have tough days and good days. On the tough days, I learn; on the good days, I live." Positive mental attitude is taking the "tough" and learning from it.

Do not confuse humility as the antithesis of positive thinking. That in itself is negative thinking. Do not assume a false modesty and say, "I am not worthy. I am not capable. I am not ready." You are molding yourself into a spiritual, social, and intellectual deformity with those thoughts.

If we are going to call ourselves children of God, then let's act like the children of a God. (Did you ever see a prince not act like a king?) Our Father in Heaven is not weak nor poor; not a failure and not incapable! He expects us to follow after Him. And with positive mental thinking, we can!

Remember, it is Satan who discourages and disheartens you. It is Satan that whispers, "You can't. You are not capable. You are not ready." Satan has power to bruise your heel, but you have power to crush his head!

A child can understand the enmity between Satan and man. When my oldest son was three, we were having a family home evening at my parents' home. Dad was giving the lesson. He asked my son the question, "Is Satan good or bad?" Jason looked at him and said without hesitation, "Bad!" Then dad asked, "Does he want to hurt you or help you?" Without hesitation again, Jason answered, "Hurt you!" Then dad asked, "What does he want to do to you?" Now came the hesitation, the intense thought, and then the flash of recognition in his three-year-old mind and eyes, and he said, "He wants to turn you into a toad!"

Your Heavenly Father loves your dearly. He knows how hard mortality is and what rancor and animosity Satan is waging against us. He hasn't abandoned us. The tools are there, the powers and the gifts. He won't let us be turned into toads! Positive mental attitude is thinking about your blessings and not your disappointments.

4. It Is Possible To Become Like God

All through the scriptures you are told to strive for perfection because all the Father has he has promised you if you'll but live

His laws. Jesus Christ set the example. He commanded us to "be ye therefore perfect."

Christ lived the perfect life. He set the example. If you were to pattern your life around his, no self-esteem would ever suffer, and you would be on your way to Godhood.

Start to work today. NOW!

List the qualities it will take to become a God:

And what is it that ye shall hope for? Behold I say unto you that ye shall have hope through the atonement of Christ and the power of his resurrection, to be raised unto life eternal, and this because of your faith in him according to the promise.

Wherefore, if a man have faith he must needs have hope; for without faith there cannot be any hope.

And again, behold I say unto you that he cannot have faith and hope, save he shall be meek, and lowly of heart.

If so, his faith and hope is vain, for none is acceptable before God, save the meek and lowly in heart; and if a man be meek and lowly in heart, and confesses by the power of the Holy Ghost that Jesus is the Christ, he must needs have charity; for if he have not charity he is nothing; wherefore he must needs have charity.

And charity suffereth long, and is kind, and envieth not, and is not puffed up, seeketh not her own, is not easily provoked, thinketh no evil, and rejoiceth not in iniquity but rejoiceth in the truth, beareth all things, believeth all things, hopeth all things, endureth all things.

Wherefore, my beloved brethren, if ye have not charity, ye are nothing, for charity never faileth. Wherefore, cleave unto charity, which is the greatest of all, for all things must fail —

But charity is the pure love of Christ, and it endureth forever; and whoso is found possessed of it at the last day, it shall be well with him.

Wherefore, my beloved brethren, pray unto the Father with all the energy of heart, that ye may be filled with this love, which he hath bestowed upon all who are true followers of his Son, Jesus Christ; that ye may become the sons of God; *that when he shall appear we shall be like him,* for we shall see him as he is; that we may have this hope; that we may be purified even as he is pure. Amen. (Moroni 7:41-48)

Did your list include:

Endurance	Charity
Meekness	Kindness
No envy	Patience (not easily provoked)
Faith	Good thoughts
Hope	No pride of the world

If you could take this list and develop each of these attributes (until you were in possession of them all) *to at least one step above what is considered "average," you would rarely experience a defeating moment.*

Now, with a Positive Mental Attitude, make a list as follows:

Why I'm Glad I'm Me (Gifts the Lord gave me)	My Opportunities To Grow (To Challenge Myself)	Godhood Qualities

The lists should be recorded in a book, journal, or diary. Writing things down helps keep a sure commitment. When you write down your thoughts, you are developing an important method of self-expression.

A woman who has spent most of her life as an educator and private tutor to handicapped children discovered some exciting concepts about keeping a journal. (And she is non-LDS.) She found that over the years, if a child (or adult) would write daily in a diary or journal, it stimulated thought process and self-expression. It wasn't at all important WHAT they wrote, only that they wrote something.

There is much more to this journal-keeping than just for historical records. The Lord is so wise. When you think a thought or idea, it can leave you or become confused as other thoughts and ideas appear. These feelings and thoughts, as they are written down — recorded — become a stable point of reference to which you can return to recapture those same thoughts, re-evaluate, and check your performance on a regular basis.

Return and report is the Lord's way. The gospel teaches us that everything that has been done on earth by Jesus Christ or ministering angels has been reported to the Father. They all have returned and reported. Journal-keeping can be this for you.

It is a place to go and vent your feelings, record your experiences, develop ideas, and be totally honest with yourself. There in those pages, admit to yourself what you really like and love about YOU. Then admit in writing what you'd like to improve upon. *You will never accomplish a goal that you haven't told yourself, "I am really going to do it."* In writing, it's a sure commitment. As you return and report, you will develop a crystal-clear picture of you, your personality, and your progress. For example:

Why I'm Glad I'm Me	My Opportunities To Grow	Godhood Qualities
I can sing	Develop my singing	Faith
I have a knack for homemaking skills	Be a better friend to my family	Hope
I am a good listener	Stop criticizing others	Charity
I have a pretty smile	Smile more	Kindness
I am friendly	Learn to control my temper	Patience
	Serve others more	Good thoughts
		No envy
		No pride
		Tenderness
		Endurance

As you look across the lists, you can see clearly where your strongest and weakest areas are and begin to set priorities on development and improvement. You can take one area and work on it for a week or a month. Each single area will have its own goals.

For example, your journal might read:

I want to learn to control my temper.
   a. Pray for strength and the Holy Ghost each morning.
   b. Repeat this goal OUT LOUD each morning and several times during the day and before bed.
   c. Force angry thoughts out of your mind.
   d. If I lose control, repent on my knees immediately.

Writing out and repeating goals out loud brings them into immediate focus and keeps them out in front of all your thoughts. As you accomplish your goals, one at a time, scratch through them with a pencil. (This can even be done on a daily basis, "I was patient all day.") It's an exhilarating feeling of success to see it crossed off forever!

It is imperative for you to accept responsibility for your self-esteem. No one or nothing can cause you unhappiness; you can only cause yourself to be unhappy. The same holds true in reverse.

Once a woman was told by a group of people that she had caused them unhappiness. Their lives were miserable because of her weaknesses. This should not be the case. Usually others cannot make us unhappy; we do it to ourselves.

As always there are exceptions to the rule, such as oppressed nations, physical abuse by others in "authority," violation of personal property, etc., but as a general rule, another individual's weakness cannot cause you personal unhappiness. You may be disappointed in that person's behavior, but to dwell on it until you become unhappy is a serious mistake. President Kimball said, "When we follow the instructions of the Lord, we are kept so busy perfecting ourselves that we come to realize that the faults of others are small in comparison." (Kimball, *Miracle of Forgiveness,* p. 269)

We cause ourselves to dwell upon the negative, adversely reasoning that if only "so and so" would stop squeezing the toothpaste in the middle, we could be happy once more! There is no time in a seventy-year-life to worry about other's faults to the point of sorrowful exhaustion. In seventy-plus years we only have enough time to control our own weaknesses and thus create personal happiness.

It is only imperfection that complains of what is imperfect. The more perfect we become, the more gentle and placid we become toward the defects of those around us.

A few years ago, I met a woman who blamed all her misfortunes on her external environment. She couldn't seem to lose weight because she was "born that way." She didn't get to college because her family hadn't given her the money. "They gave it to the other children but not to me." She was highly critical of others' successes because she just had "bad luck." This woman was seriously unhappy. There really and truly is a reason some people seem to make it and others never do.

You have heard the excuses, and probably at least once in your life said one of them to yourself. All of the following are examples of negative thinking:

1. *Blaming family or environment.* "It's my family's fault." "I came from the wrong side of the tracks." "What do you expect from me, look at my family." "People reject me because I'm poor."

2. *Blaming events.* "I only have bad luck." "Sure she's a success, she's lucky." "The weather prevented me from doing it."

3. *Labeling.* "I am a lonely person." "I am a depressed person." I had a roommate in college that started every morning with the statement, "Oh, I am so depressed." She made me depressed. Whether we label ourselves or accept someone else's label of us, we are using a crutch.

4. *Blaming others.* "He hurt me." "The bishop fouled it up." "She insulted me, so I quit."

5. *Excusing our behavior.* "I was born this way." "This is inherited. My mom is just like this." "Well, everybody else does it." "Satan made me do it." "I am not organized." "I was sick."

The Lord has made everyone a free agent, and no test is given to you that you do not have the power to control. What excuses can you tell Him? I didn't get my genealogy done because I was sick. I was a lonely person on earth, so I didn't meet anyone to whom I could teach the gospel. I couldn't pay my tithing because my husband was too lazy to find a decent-paying job. Etc., etc., etc.

We have the free agency to act for ourselves. "All truth is independent in that sphere in which God has placed it, to act for itself, as all intelligence also; otherwise there is no existence." (D & C 99:30)

Next time you feel an excuse coming on, square back your shoulders and listen for the voice: "Hey, you're not going to get away with that!"

Honestly tell yourself the real reasons for your flaws and behavior. It is painful to be honest. But until you are frank enough with yourself, you cannot fully progress. Why? Because you block the thought process necessary to produce change. You block it because it prevents that pain of honesty. It hurts to admit you are wrong, or have been unrighteous. It really hurts. But I submit to you, until you accept the responsibility for your self-esteem and actions, you can only settle into the stagnant comfort of complacency. Until you suffer the pain sufficient to produce change, you simply stagnate.

I don't believe anyone who has stagnated has yet made it to Godhood.

Chapter  Two

Develop Your Identity — Spiritually

Now that you know who you are, what are you going to do about it?

Daughters of kings and queens are taught to act like their parents in order to fulfill a role as a potential queen. As a daughter of God, you too are promised a potential role as a goddess. Knowing who you are and esteeming yourself as an offspring of a God helps you in determining how you should develop your identity and self-worth. The first and most important is your spiritual development.

"Therefore, what manner of men ought ye to be? Verily I say unto you, even as I am." (3 Nephi 27:27)

What manner of woman ought ye to be? As Jesus Christ himself is, you are told. *What one single thing makes the personality of Jesus so desirable?* We know He is kind, gentle, pure in heart, humble, and obedient. But the single quality that He possesses that causes us to revere Him so deeply is His UNCONDITIONAL LOVE FOR ALL MANKIND. He suffered, bled, and then died for all, not just for the members of His Church, or the Jews, or any select group. He put no conditions on WHO He died for, only on those who could enter His Kingdom.

As the crucifiers proceeded with their awful task, not unlikely with roughness and taunts, for killing was their trade and to scenes of anguish they had grown callous through long familiarity, the agonized Sufferer, void of resentment but full of pity for their heartlessness and capacity for cruelty, voiced the first of the seven utterances delivered from the cross. In the spirit of God-like mercy He prayed: 'Father, forgive them; for they know not what they do.' . . . Jesus looking with tender compassion upon His weeping mother, as she stood with John at the foot of the cross, commended her to the care and protection of the beloved disciple, with the words, 'Woman, behold thy son!' and to John, 'Behold thy mother!' (Talmage, *Jesus the Christ*, pp. 655-656, 660)

Even at the end, He showed no concern for Himself. It was for His mother and her well-being and even for His crucifiers that He showed concern. There are those you know in mortal life for whom you hold unconditional love — for example, your children or parents or other loved ones. You may hate the sin, but you don't hate the sinner. How do you develop such love for all mankind, such charity?

In order to develop that kind of love, to live and be like Christ Himself, even to begin to get there, you must first love yourself — learn to esteem YOU.

You must take what you know of your origin and develop a communication and relationship with the Father. When these channels are opened, you begin to feel an intervening spirit in your behalf. You begin to feel comfort and encouragement and you begin to feel secure in His love for you. As a Latter-day Saint, only then can your love for yourself begin to bud and blossom and bloom.

There are certain fundamental steps to developing that relationship with the Father. Many LDS women take their problems, anxieties, and frustrations to their Bishop, home teacher, husband, or other priesthood leader. They lean heavily on the advice of others. They listen as the Bishop admonishes them to seek the Lord's counsel. But in action, women tend to depend too heavily on this mortal relationship. The secret is not to become dependent on a Bishop or a husband, but to become dependent on the Lord. A priesthood leader may counsel and advise, but he should not be depended upon to run your life or make your decisions or stand as the liaison between you and the Father. You are the one who must take it up with your Father.

The prophet Joseph Smith in "Instructions to the Women of the Church" said:

> If you neglect the duties devolving upon you and depend on the Prophet, you will be darkened in your mind. Depend on no man, or men, for a righteous person can only deliver his own soul. *(Documentary History of the Church IV*, pp. 602-607)

He also said:

> I have known individuals who have trembled at the idea of passing through certain ordeals who after they were through the temptation said they could approach the Lord *in more confidence* and ask for such blessings as they desired. Every man has got to learn to stand upon his own knowledge; he cannot depend upon his neighbor; every man must be independent; he must depend upon his God for himself entirely. It depends upon himself to see if he will stand the tide of trouble and overcome the impediments that are strewed in the pathway of life to prevent his progress. (Gems of Truth, *Millenial Star*, p. 806, December 10, 1888.)

When you pass the test, you KNOW you are worthy and can come to the Lord in *confidence*. The relationship we have with the Father puts us in a situation to advance in knowledge. We know He has told us we are responsible for our own actions. He has given us a plan and rules and laws which to follow that will test our obedience. By being obedient, we draw closer to Him, and He to us, and instead of being "darkened" in the mind, we are enlightened. Light is knowledge. Increase in knowledge comes after the relationship is established. Increased knowledge assures us of who we are, why we're here, and where we are going. All are essentials to a healthy self-esteem.

Heber C. Kimball said:

> The time is coming when no man or woman will be able to endure on borrowed light. Each will have to be guided by the light within himself. If you do not have it you will not stand. (*Conference Reports*, October 1955, p. 56)

Well, how do you, as a busy woman, begin this process of revitalizing your relationship with the Father?

1. *Prayer and the Holy Ghost.* This is the number one key. How much have you read and heard about the power of prayer? Elder Groberg of the First Quorum of Seventy admonished in a stake conference to just add ten minutes a day to what prayers you offered. If you prayed two minutes in the morning and three minutes at night, just add five more minutes to each prayer. Why? Through sincere and efficacious prayer, you can feel an intervening spirit and influence. It would be the same as if you called your mortal father on the phone each morning and evening, said "Hello," and then hung up. How could you know what he was thinking, or any advice he might offer, or how would he know of your needs and feelings? In prayer, you must learn to be specific in thanking and asking. And you must learn to "talk" to Him as you would talk to your own earthly father. Tell Him of your joys and sorrows, your failures and accomplishments, your goals and ideas, your plans and cancellations. Let Him become involved in your life. You can involve Him. He really is your best friend, and He really is listening. He really does want to help and sustain you. But He is bound by certain laws; unless you live by those laws, He can't help you. Unless you ask, He can't answer.

One of the specifics that needs to be asked for and lived for is the *constant* companionship of the Holy Ghost.

How important is the Holy Ghost in your daily life? Is he even there? How often does he prompt and influence you? Exactly what is his role?

Let us continue with the rest of Parley P. Pratt's thought on man as God in embryo:

> An intelligent being in the image of God, possesses every organ, attribute, sense, sympathy, affection that is possessed by God Himself. . .The gift of the Holy Ghost adapts itself to all these organs or attributes. It quickens all the intellectual faculties, increases, enlarges, expands and purifies all the natural passions and affections. . . .It inspires, develops, cultivates, and matures all the fine-toned sympathies, joys, tastes, kindred feelings, and affections of our nature. It inspires virtue, kindness, goodness, tenderness, gentleness, and charity. It develops beauty of person, form, and feature. It tends to health, vigor, animation, and social feeling. It invigorates all the faculties to the physical and intellectual man. It strengthens, and gives tone to the nerves. . .marrow to the bone, joy to the heart, light to the eyes, music to the ears, and life to the whole being. (*Key to Theology,* p. 101)

How important is the Holy Ghost in your DAILY life? HE IS CRITICALLY IMPORTANT!

If every man possesses every organ and attribute that God himself possesses, but in the "rough," how does man perfect those organs and attributes (the physical and the spiritual) so that he may become like God?

The gift of the Holy Ghost adapts itself to all these organs or attributes. The word *adapts* means the Holy Ghost has the power to come to man's level and aid man as the propelling vehicle that carries man from his rudimentary state to Godhood.

How can He do that?

He quickens all the intellectual faculties, increases, enlarges, expands and purifies all the natural passions and affections. He helps you understand your potential (quickens all the intellectual faculties). He helps you understand and control your natural passions (eating, sex, sleep, etc.) and purifies them.

He inspires, develops, cultivates, and matures all the fine-toned sympathies, joys, tastes, kindred feelings and affections of our nature. The Holy Ghost inspires you in re-remembering the "nature" of your spirit — the "kind" of spirit you are. He helps you to recall who you were and what your talents were before you came to earth life (fine-toned sympathies, joys, tastes and affections of our nature). He helps you develop your talents. As you understand and cultivate the "nature" of your spirit, you are prompted by the Holy Ghost with kindred feelings toward others, even toward other things. When I hear gospel teachings, I know I've heard them before. Toward some of my friends and loved ones I feel such kindred feelings. I know I knew them before I came to earth. (I also find it significant that we are taught to search out our "kindred" dead.) The Holy ghost helped me recognize these "kindred" feelings. He can touch your heart and whisper to your ear of things that the veil has temporarily made obscure. He crystallizes that dimmed vision into perfect clarity.

The Holy Ghost *inspires virtue, kindness, goodness, tenderness, gentleness, and charity.*

> If so, his faith and hope is vain, for none is acceptable before God, save the meek and lowly in heart; and if a man be meek and lowly in heart, and confesses by the power of the Holy Ghost that Jesus is the Christ, he must needs have charity; for if he have not charity he is nothing; wherefore he must needs have charity.
>
> And charity suffereth long, and is kind, and envieth not, and is not puffed up, seeketh not her own, is not easily provoked, thinketh no evil, and rejoiceth not in iniquity but rejoiceth in the truth, beareth all things, believeth all things, hopeth all things, endureth all things. (Moroni 7:44-45)

Even before earth life, our nature was not like God's. We needed to come to earth to take those rough attributes and polish them until smooth. By the power of the Holy Ghost, you can gain the pure love of Christ and the personality of Jesus Christ Himself.

The Holy Ghost *develops beauty of person, form, and feature.* Some time ago, there was an employee of mine who was Jewish, who asked me, "What is it about you Mormons? You all have this 'clean' look about you. Is it a special soap you use or something?" It was that "or something" I had to explain!

There is something that happens that is a literal change, even to the point of beauty in the countenance of the individual. Even here, it is evident how the Holy Ghost is the vehicle to enable man to perfect himself. (Adapt itself to all these organs.)

> And now behold, I ask of you, my brethren of the church, have ye spiritually been born of God? *Have ye received his image in your countenances?* Have ye experienced this mighty change in your hearts? (Alma 5:14)

The Holy Ghost *tends to health, vigor, animation, and social feeling.* He can inspire you to controlling your mind as to physical ailments and fatigue. Physicians are now saying that over 85 percent of illnesses (not diseases) are caused by "thinking" about them, by giving in to psychosomatic thoughts. With enough self-discipline and the companionship of the Holy Ghost to inspire that physical control, you can be healthier. The Holy Ghost will aid you in developing more personality, animation, and social feeling in your social life and social encounters. The companionship of the Holy Ghost gives you self-confidence.

The Holy Ghost *invigorates all the faculties of the physical and intellectual man.* A friend once said, "Joseph Smith was the most intelligent man of the 19th Century." What did that mean? Did my friend believe that this man with very little schooling was THE most intelligent man? Certainly there were brilliant men and great minds at this time, but Joseph was THE most intelligent man of the 19th Century because he was taught by the Holy Ghost. You can only gain entrance to the Celestial Kingdom *after* you have been taught by the Holy Ghost.

The Prophet Joseph Smith said:

> A person may profit by noticing the first intimation of the spirit of revelation; for instance, when you feel pure intelligence flowing into you, it may give you sudden strokes of ideas, so that by noticing it, you may find it fulfilled the same day or soon; (i.e.)

36

those things that were presented unto your minds by the Spirit of God, will come to pass; and thus by learning the Spirit of God and understanding it, you may grow into the principle of revelation, until you become perfect in Christ Jesus. (*Teachings of the Prophet Joseph Smith,* p. 151)

The Holy Ghost is that Pure Intelligence flowing through you. We often quote D & C 93:36: "The Glory of God is intelligence." But we don't finish the sentence, "or, in other words, light and truth." Light and truth are the Holy Ghost, that "pure intelligence flowing unto you. . . ," that education you receive by the Spirit. Joseph Smith had that understanding of intelligence. His mind, body, and spirit were taught and quickened by the Holy Ghost.

In Moroni 10:4-5, verse four concerns the people who are not members of the Church. Verse five is for the members of the Church: "And by the power of the Holy Ghost, ye may know the truth of *all* things."

A young man having joined the Church, bore this testimony: "I'll tell you why I joined this Church. I came to a time in my life when my heart told me things that my mind did not know."

When we understand more than we know with our minds, when we understand with our hearts, then the spirit of the Lord is working with us.

Concerning the Savior's visit to the Nephites:

> And tongue cannot speak the words which he prayed, neither can be written by man the words which he prayed.
>
> And the multitude did hear and do bear record; and their hearts were open and they did understand in their hearts the words which he prayed.
>
> Nevertheless, so great and marvelous were the words which he prayed that they cannot be written, neither can they be uttered by man. (3 Nephi 19:32-34)

Were the words he spoke so unusual or sacred that they couldn't be written down? No. There are things that can be understood only by the Spirit through the heart. There is a level of understanding in the heart that exceeds that of the mind.

The Holy Ghost *strengthens, and gives tone to the nerves. . . marrow to the bone. . . .* The Holy Ghost is the First Comforter. He can calm you and soften you. He can arm you with strength in the face of trials and discouragement. He can actually cause a renewing of the body. "For whoso is faithful unto. . .the magnifying their calling, are sanctified by the Spirit unto the renewing of their bodies." (D & C 84:33) It is through this sanctifying that a literal change occurs. Marrow is a literal substance in the body. The Spirit renews this strength within us. How else can men in their old age fly around the world, put in countless hours, and lead this Church for the Lord?

He gives *joy to the heart, light to the eyes, music to the ears, and life to the whole being.* The Holy Ghost is the key to self-esteem (joy to the heart), and light to the eyes, and a genuinely good feeling about your life's existence and work on earth (life to the whole being)!

Sisters, how important is the Holy Ghost to you? He is THE most important VEHICLE you have in developing all those attributes described by Elder Pratt. What is a vehicle? It is something that takes you from one place to another, from rudimentary man to perfect Godhood. You cannot progress in self-esteem or discover or be taught about yourself and your talents unless you are seeking the Holy Ghost and then listening to Him.

How do you hear Him? Is it a dramatic experience when he communicates?

We read about Elijah, the Prophet. He needed to hear from the Lord. He waited. And then:

> . . .the Lord passed by, and a great and strong wind rent the mountains, and brake in pieces the rocks before the Lord; but the Lord was not in the wind; and after the wind an earthquake; but the Lord was not in the earthquake:

> And after the earthquake a fire; but the Lord was not in the
> fire: and after the fire a still small voice. (1 Kings 19:11-12)

A short time ago, my husband, in the capacity of his calling, was interviewing a man who had been excommunicated. This man told him that, "I never realized how much the Holy Ghost influenced my life until He was taken away."

This had an overwhelming effect on me. Having been baptized at age eight, I never really knew life without the Holy Ghost. Here was an individual who was seeing life without it, after once having the gift.

So I began an experiment. For a few days I gave strict attention to all the thoughts and ideas that came to my mind. I would ask myself, was this my own thought or was this the Holy Ghost? It was amazing to me how much He really did influence me on a day-to-day basis, and it was amazingly easy to discern Him once I paid attention.

He is there, the still small voice, the reassurance, if we will just listen. The statements made by Parley P. Pratt are clear and descriptive of the power of the Holy Ghost if we just learn to live by the Spirit. He will enlighten you, teach you, and help you to develop all your talents and attributes.

> And the light which shineth, which giveth you light, is
> through him who enlighteneth your eyes, which is the same light
> that quickenth your understandings; (D & C 88:11)

To be taught by the Spirit, you must live to be worthy of revelation. You must be obedient to God's commandments and demonstrate self-discipline. The Apostle Paul told us to grieve not the Spirit lest we lose it.

> And grieve not the holy Spirit of God, whereby ye are sealed
> unto the day of redemption.

> Let all bitterness, and wrath, and anger, and clamour, and evil
> speaking, be put away from you, with all malice:

And be ye kind one to another, tenderhearted, forgiving one another, even as God for Christ's sake hath forgiven you. (Ephesians 4:30-32)

"When you have the Spirit:

1. You feel happy, calm, and clear-minded.
2. You feel generous.
3. Nobody can offend you.
4. You wouldn't mind everybody seeing what you're doing.
5. You are eager to be with people and want to make them happy.
6. You are glad when others succeed.
7. You are glad to attend your meetings and participate in church activities.
8. You feel like praying.
9. You wish you could keep all the Lord's commandments.
10. You feel "in control." You don't overeat or sleep too much; you don't feel uncontrollably drawn to sensational enter-tainment, lose your temper, or feel uncontrollable passions or desires.
11. You think about the Savior often and lovingly; you want to know him better.
12. You feel confident and are glad to be alive.

"When you don't have the Spirit:

1. You feel unhappy, depressed, confused, and frustrated.
2. You feel possessive, self-centered, or resentful of demands made on you.
3. You are easily offended.
4. You become secretive and evasive.
5. You avoid people, especially members of your family; and you are critical of family members and Church authorities.
6. You envy or resent the successes of others.
7. You don't want to go to church, go home teaching, or take the sacrament. You wish you had another church job or no job at all.
8. You don't want to pray.
9. You find the commandments bothersome, restricting, or senseless.

10. You feel emotions and appetites so strongly that you fear you cannot control them: hate, jealousy, anger, lust, hunger, fatigue.
11. You hardly ever think of the Savior; he seems irrelevant to your life, or worse, part of a confusing system that seems to work against you.
12. You get discouraged easily and wonder if life is really worth it. (*Ensign*, August 1978, pp. 32-33)

2. Read the Scriptures Daily. Not once a week or even every other day, but daily. Why?

The first and most basic reason is the immediate self-esteem that will result because you mastered the self-discipline required to read them every day. Constantly, you are being instructed to read the scriptures every day. When you can say, "Yes, I do read them every day," you feel that surge of self-worth and esteem. The obvious other benefits come after. You will hunger and thirst after more knowledge. Your spiritual and intellectual development will increase through the gift of the Holy Ghost, and you will begin to understand concepts in such depth, your whole being will be electrified.

There is something eternal to us in those words. We heard them before; they are familiar to us. As we read them every day, the veil becomes thinner and we can "feel" back to where home really is. If you could see how great you were before you came here, your self-mastery and self-esteem would never be in question. Reading those words brings you closer to feeling that greatness.

There is much to be learned by other's mistakes, much to be gained by words of counsel, and much to be cherished by knowing through those scriptures the love the Savior and the Father have for you.

> It's no longer a question of whether you have been through the standard works, but whether the life and light in them has somehow passed through the very skin of your bodies and enlivened you. (Truman Madsen, *Highest in Us,* p. 26)

41

3. *Live Righteously.* Repent of your weaknesses and recommit yourself *daily* to obey the commandments. The questions asked for the temple recommend can help you evaluate your state of life.

(a) If you have ever been involved in a transgression relating to the law of chastity, was it resolved by the proper priesthood authority?

(b) Do you earnestly strive to do your duty in the Church by attending Relief Society, Sacrament Meeting, etc.?

(c) Do you sustain the other local and general authorities of the Church?

(d) Do you pay a full tithing?

(e) Are you totally honest in your dealings with your fellow men?

(f) Do you live the Word of Wisdom?

(g) Do you earnestly try to live in accordance with all of the accepted rules and doctrines of the Church?

(h) If you have been through the temple, do you wear the regulation garments both night and day?

(i) If there has been anything amiss in your life, was it resolved with the proper priesthood authorities?

Your answers to the questions should all be yes. But if they are not, start today to change what you are doing so that you will feel better about yourself. If you have a problem or weakness that you want to overcome, get down on your knees as soon as you have finished reading this section, tell the Lord you have the problem, tell Him how you honestly feel about it, tell Him of the frustration, ask Him to forgive you, and make a commitment to Him to overcome this, ask for His help and support, repent, and pour out your heart to Him. Then go to your "secret place" and record your feelings and write down your commitment. If necessary — for moral transgressions — go to your proper priesthood authority (Bishop, etc.). Then forsake that sin or weakness! Just go out and "sin no more." Sound too easy? It's not often easy to get the mind to the state of a "broken heart and contrite spirit." Usually, by that point, you've sinned once too many times. Then the feelings of self-worth are at their lowest. But once the commitment to change what you're doing is there, it can be easy. Pray, keep the commandments, record and evaluate your thoughts and progress, counsel with your husband or Bishop, if necessary, but above all, counsel with the Lord.

4. *Service.* "When ye are in the service of your fellow beings ye are only in the service of your God." (Mosiah 2:17)

A friend once said:

> Whenever I get depressed, I've learned the secret of extirpating that depression. First, I realize that being depressed is purely selfish, with only thoughts of myself; I am at my most selfish moment. Second, I concentrate immediately on someone else's needs and serve them. I have discovered each time that I do this, the depression immediately leaves, I feel an inner warmth, renewed vitality and peace with God.

Service is a necessary step to develop your self-esteem. Without it, you cannot even begin the process of becoming like God. A wonderful example was set by the Savior himself as he washed the feet of His disciples:

> So after he had washed their feet, . . .he said unto them, Know ye what I have done to you?
>
> Ye call me Master and Lord: and ye say well; for so I am.
>
> If I then, your Lord and Master, have washed your feet; ye also ought to wash one another's feet.
>
> For I have given you an example, that ye should do as I have done to you.
>
> Verily, verily, I say unto you, The servant is not greater than his Lord; neither he that is sent greater than he that sent him.
>
> If ye know these things, happy are ye if ye do them. (John 13:12-17)

This is what my friend had discovered. Serving others brought her happiness. It brought her closer to the pure love of Christ, and this, in turn, brought her closer to Him. She felt that intervening spirit and His love for her. This kind of accomplishment is the richest experience in self-worth.

> Wherefore, my beloved brethren, *if ye have not charity, ye are nothing,* for charity never faileth. Wherefore, cleave unto charity, which is the greatest of all, for all things must fail—
>
> But charity is the pure love of Christ, and it endureth forever; and whoso is found possessed of it at the last day, it shall be well with him.
>
> Wherefore, my beloved brethren, pray unto the Father with all the energy of heart, that ye may be filled with this love, which he hath bestowed upon all who are true followers of his Son, Jesus Christ; that ye may become the sons of God; that when he shall appear we shall be like him, for we shall see him as he is; that we may have this hope; that we may be purified even as he is pure. Amen. (Moroni 7:46-48)

If you don't understand what charity is, if you don't seek it, if you don't have it, you will never have the fullness of self-esteem.

"If ye have not charity, ye are nothing."

Charity is a gift, "the greatest of all," that has been given to you; it is not acquired, but rather, developed.

Charity is "the pure love of Christ," or in other words, unconditional love for your fellow beings. We are commanded to seek after the personality of the Savior, to become like Him. He had *great* self-esteem. Remember what Alma asked? "Have ye received His image in your countenances?" (Alma 5:14)

Without charity, without unconditional love for mankind, we cannot have the fullness of self-esteem or become like Him, ". . .that ye may be filled with this love. . .that when He shall appear we shall be like Him." Read those verses over and over.

In the January 1979 issue of the *Ensign*, there is an inspiring story of a woman who made a resolution to perform an act of love or service 365 days a year. It is wonderful! Read it. Although it is a difficult goal (I know, I tried it and failed.), the concepts are there to be learned whether on a daily or weekly basis. This woman found that she came away from a visit with much more than she had taken. In her words:

> As the year has progressed, I have come to realize that charity is not always convenient, and that it sometimes takes much thought and planning. At first, I was proud of all the 'good' I was doing, but as the year comes to an end, I am humbled to realize how selfish I have been all my life. As I left the home of the bedridden, or listened to frustrated teenagers, or climbed the hills with my children, I often thought of all the lives I could have touched in previous years if only I had taken the time. My one consulation is knowing that I can make a similar journey in this coming year, and in all the years ahead.
>
> Let thy bowels also be full of charity towards all men. . .then shall thy *confidence* wax strong. . . (D & C 121:45)

Charity is not merely an act of kindness or compassion, but it is a whole way of life, the Savior's life.

Elder Vaughn Featherstone tells the story of how he was impressed with the meaning of charity — the pure love of Christ:

> The truth of that concept was impressed upon my mind some years ago when I was on the Priesthood Missionary Committee of the Church and had the privilege of being assigned to a stake conference in Pocatello, Idaho, with President Marion G. Romney, who at that time was a member of the Council of the Twelve. Between sessions of conference we went outside to get some fresh air. We walked several times around the parking lot; then President Romney stopped and said to me, 'Brother Featherstone, do you think the brethren of the Priesthood will ever come to understand that they were born to serve their fellowmen?' That question has had a profound impact on my life. (Vaughn Featherstone, *Charity Never Faileth*, p. 8)

He goes on to say:

Charity is a total submission to the Savior's will. It is the total commitment of the soul. When the Holy Ghost pervades every particle of our being, we are filled with an awe and respect for all God's creations, even to the lowliest form of animal life. Much of that which we supposed was 'sport' no longer has excitement or pleasure.

And if we have such marvelous respect for God's creation, shall we not stand in absolute wonder at a man, a woman, or a child? Charity may cause us to detest what they do, but we can never cease to strive with them. We can look to their faults and be patient and forgiving because charity suffereth long and is kind. We forgive offenses, realizing that to forgive is a divine communication. . .It means that we make ourselves totally available for service, that we realize we were born to serve our fellowmen. . . (Vaughn Featherstone, *Charity Never Faileth*, pp. 5-6)

Developing charity increases our self-esteem because, by a quite natural process, we wax strong in confidence, because we know instinctively (re-remembering) we are successful at what we were born to do!

It is important to mention forgiveness in consideration with charity. Forgiveness is a commandment. "I, the Lord, will forgive whom I will forgive, but of you it is required to forgive all men." (D & C 64:10)

To harbor anger or hate or bitterness toward any individual is to canker the soul. An unforgiving mind is like an open wound which burns, throbs, stings with pain. It cannot close itself and excretes poisons and pus until the whole spirit is infected. "Whosoever hateth his brother is a murderer: and ye know that no murderer hath eternal life abiding in him." (I John 3:15)

Usually, the person who is hated doesn't even know how bitter and strong the hatred against him (or her) is. It is the one who hates that suffers, laying awake at night, mentally fatigued with thoughts of vituperation, verbally degrading his enemy and making others wearisome of the assaults. The damage comes to the one who hates.

46

Forgiveness is forgetting. Henry Ward Beecher said: "I can forgive but I cannot forget is another way of saying I cannot forgive."

President Kimball said:

> Many people, when brought to a reconciliation with others, say that they forgive, but they continue to hold malice, continue to suspect the other party, continue to disbelieve the other's sincerity. This is sin, for when a reconciliation has been effected and when repentance is claimed, each should forgive and forget. . . (Spencer W. Kimball, *Miracle of Forgiveness*, pp. 262-263)

Forgiveness is also silence. When you have been offended or transgressed, to broadcast or share the offense with others is not forgiveness. To scathe others publicly for their sin is equally as offensive to God as is the sin committed. It is not the Lord's way. Revenge also belongs only to the Lord. (See Romans 12:19.)

Ask yourself, do I want to take on the personality of Jesus Christ? If your answer is yes, then ask, "Would He forgive?" As He hung on the cross, remember what He said?

Forgiveness is not judging.

> And why beholdest thou the mote that is in thy brother's eye, but considerest not the beam that is in thine own eye?
>
> Or how wilt thou say to thy brother, Let me pull out the mote out of thine eye; and, behold, a beam is in thine own eye? (Matthew 7:3-4)

> This should leave no doubt in any mind. The unequalness of the beam and the mote is telling. A mote is a tiny sliver like a small portion from a toothpick, while the beam is usually a great, strong timber or metal which runs from wall to wall to support the heavy roof of the building. When one is loaded down with the beam-size weaknesses and sins, it is certainly wrong to forget his own difficult position while he makes mountains of the molehill-size errors of his brother. (Spencer W. Kimball, *Miracle of Forgiveness*, p. 269)

There is a contentious woman who hates her husband's ex-wife. It has all ensued from past hostilities, competition, and resentments. Now it has reached colossal proportion. She has accused the ex-wife unjustly, borne false witness, incited contention, and influenced her husband and families into animosity. Now the couple together hold malice, suspect every action of the ex-wife, and continue to disbelieve her sincerity. They have accused her of harboring evil thoughts, immorality, dishonesty, vanity, and usery. Certainly the ex-wife would seem justified in finding disgust and repugnance against this couple, especially towards the woman. What should she do? She knows that the Lord will not allow those feelings to be excused.

> For if ye forgive men their trespasses, your Heavenly Father will also forgive you:
>
> But if ye forgive not men their trespasses, neither will your Father forgive your trespasses. (Matthew 6:14-15)

However, it wasn't easy to find forgiveness in her heart for them. At first, she tried to defend herself. Then she wanted to fight back. She found herself one day reading Alma 41:14 where he says be careful what you send out for it will come back to you. In her heart she was gratified to read this, thinking "they would get what they deserved." But instantly, another scripture flashed through her mind: "for there remaineth in him the greater sin," (D & C 64:9). She knew she was wrong. So in full repentance, overwhelmed with a spirit of remorse and restitution for such anger and feelings, she knelt and begged forgiveness from her Father in Heaven. A sweet spirit settled her thoughts, and she has had peace from that moment on. There are times when it is trying for her, and Satan attempts to manipulate her thoughts, but she falls to her knees and re-establishes the repentance and forgiveness process. In that process, she also asks the Lord to forgive them.

You must be free too in order to progress. You must forgive them: father, mother, brother, sister, ex-spouse, husband, child, friend, neighbor, leader, associate, whomever. Forgive and forget.

If you at present have any feelings of hate or anger or bitterness to any individual, you are not living as you should. You should be seeking forgiveness from the Lord. You cannot progress to your full potential until you do.

Chapter  Three

Develop Your Identity — Physically

"**C**ease to be idle. . . .cease to sleep longer than is needful; retire to thy bed early, that ye may not be weary; arise early, that you bodies and your minds may be invigorated." (D & C 88:124)

And in the 89th Section of the *Doctrine and Covenants* is the Word of Wisdom as outlined by the Lord, and He concludes those words by saying:

> And all saints who remember to keep and do these sayings, walking in obedience to the commandments, shall receive health in their naval and marrow to their bones;
>
> And shall find wisdom and *great treasures of knowledge, even hidden treasures;*
>
> And shall run and not be weary, and shall walk and not faint. (verses 18-20)

Now that you have identified yourself and have established goals to gain spiritual self-worth, what about this mortal package in which your spirit is wrapped? Spiritual growth and communication is the number one and first essential step for the Latter-day Saint woman to gain a healthy self-esteem. But no matter how superb your spirit feels, if you don't feel good about your body or appearance — or worse, if you don't care — you cannot have a good self-image. This is true no matter what life has given you in the way of physical handicaps, flaws, and imperfections. Even with severe physical handicaps, you can feel good about your body and appearance. The physical self is a reflection of the inner self. How you feel about *you* shows on the outside.

Constantly, and in conjunction with the commandments in the scriptures, we are being admonished to take care of this tabernacle of flesh, to maintain good diets and regular exercise. Yet women in the Church have voiced the following (selected) excuses:

"Oh, I'm always pregnant."

"There wasn't enough time in between babies."

"I'm thinking about getting pregnant."

"You know, they say with every baby it's worse."

"With all this work, who has time?"

"No time to eat regularly; we all have different schedules."

"I was born this way."

"There's no hope for me."

"I've always been fat."

"I hate dressing up; it's uncomfortable."

"I have more important things to do."

"Who has time for makeup? It takes too long to put on."

"I don't have the money."

Any of these sound familiar? They are excuses, and, according to the scriptures, excuses just don't count! In today's modern world, with such an emphasis on grooming and fashion, can the women of the Church stand as a beacon light to all the other women of the world if they are not in command of their appearance?

Not only are good health and good grooming essential for our self-respect and self-image, it is vital to our capacity to influence others, family, friends, and the outside world.

Aren't we a member missionary church? Aren't we fighting against issues such as abortion, ERA, sterility clinics, pornography, etc.? How can we carry any force or impact if we don't appear as self-confident, attractive, and intelligent women?

One distinguished gentleman observing Mormon women noted that those he saw around him "are overweight and trying to hide it in long flowering mu-mus." Is this true? Observe around you, observe yourself. Can you improve?

There is no excuse for a sloppy appearance, even at home — maybe I should say *especially* at home. When your family observes you, what are you saying about yourself to them in your appearance? If your hair is unkempt and oily, or your clothes wrinkled and soiled, and you wear no makeup or show no sparkle, what are they learning by your example? Do you only dress up to go out? Is that not dishonesty? For whom are you trying to look nice? If an important dignitary were to come to your home, would you look as nice as you could for the visit? If the Savior were to come, would you change your appearance? You and then your family are the most important people you know. To present an insipid and banal appearance is to acknowledge a lack of self-respect.

More often than not, I hear the excuse, "I have more important things to do. It just isn't important to me." This is such a dishonest assessment of the inadequacies these women feel in grooming themselves. Whenever I (or others) have given a mini-class on any facet of personal grooming such as makeup technique, clothes, etc., the classes have been jammed, standing room only. Women want to know what to do; they want to feel good about their personal appearance. I have discovered that when they simply don't know how, and are afraid to experiment, they make up the excuses.

How important should good grooming be among your list of priorities? It should be second next to spirituality. Caring to flatter the physical body is not vanity. I believe it is an inborn trait, perhaps coming from prior training from our Mother in Heaven. I am sure she is meticulous about her appearance. She taught us well, and it feels familiar to us, this wanting to be feminine and lovely creatures. It is weakness that causes you to overlook or shun that responsibility. Why is it a responsibility? Because you are a daughter of a God; you must represent Him here on earth. Because you are an influence, by natural birthright, on lives around you. Because the inside can't fully sparkle when the outside shine has become tarnished by apathetic neglect.

When your external appearance reflects a lack-luster attitude, your circle of influence diminishes. I could be the greatest designer in the world, but if I am a sloppy, overweight, disheveled person, to whom can I sell an idea about good taste? If that is your personal external image, to whom can you sell a good idea, to whom can you sell the gospel, to whom can you influence towards positive change? Yes, a few perhaps, but not with the impact a neat, clean, smart-looking woman could.

It is the same principle the Church has about sending the missionaries out into the field as well-groomed, clean-cut representatives of the Lord.

You must also accept the things you cannot change. If you have physical handicaps or deformities or flaws that can't be corrected (large hips, short legs, etc.), please don't complain. There is nothing you can do to change these, but you can make the best of it. You can still look pretty and feel good about yourself by taking a positive point of view and making your assets (pretty smile, loving eyes, gorgeous hair) your most important features! You do this with the help of the following suggestions:

Money, time, schedules, pregnancies have nothing to do with weight control, exercise, and good grooming. In fact, it's cheaper to eat less, exercise is free, and soap, shampoo, and a good iron are very inexpensive! The secret is self-discipline, which will be discussed thoroughly in the next chapter.

There are hundreds of diets and exercise plans, and perhaps thousands of beauty aids, cosmetics, and like products. There are styles, and fashions, and fads to choose from. Where do you begin?

1. *With Proper Diet.* Through your Relief Society, County Extension Service, or local library, you can find literature on the five basic food groups and plan nutritious and delightful meals for you and the family. It's not hard; it only takes self-discipline.

If you are overweight, you need to begin a controlled diet. (If you have special medical problems, do it under a doctor's care.) There are diets that are all eggs, all fruit, all water, etc. These are fads or crash diets and don't teach you self-control. How did you get overweight in the beginning? Overeating, especially the wrong foods. Now you may temporarily lose weight by eating eggs and water, but after the diet, what? You are pretty tired of eggs. Good eating habits should be established immediately, and a successful diet (one where you lose and it stays lost) is usually started by *changing eating habits.*

You need to be conscious of counting calories in the beginning. As boring and regimental as it is, there is no other way. You just have to make up your mind, write it down, keep a daily journal, and report often to yourself of your progress.

When I was 18, my weight was 140 pounds on a 5'2" frame. I only fooled myself in thinking, "Oh, you're only a few pounds overweight." *When I made the commitment to lose the weight, I made it for the rest of my life.* Never again would I be fat. So there came the boring days of counting calories and controlling eating habits. My weight has been maintained at 100 pounds for the last 16 years, even through three pregnancies. It is because I made that commitment for life, not until the weight came off. I know a woman who was obese all her life. Finally, lacking the self-discipline to do it on her own, she went to a weight control clinic, lived ten months on liquid protein, and spent over $2,000. She looked terrific! Six months later, she had gained back half of what she'd lost! Why? The commitment was only until she lost the weight. She really didn't want to do it on her own, or she would have! Can you imagine how her self-esteem suffered after this, another failure?

Note: One secret I learned long ago: Weigh yourself every morning. Those extra pounds can't "sneak" up on you then. You can do something about it that very day!

2. *Regular Exercise.* Again, there are as many exercises and exercise programs as there are wonder diets. Exercise is critical, not so much for losing weight or weight control, but for muscle tone and good circulation. The heart is a muscle and must be exercised so that it may maintain strength and keep the blood circulating properly throughout the body. Getting oxygen to the organs (oxygen is carried by the blood) is also critical for keeping those vital organs in tone. Any form of stimulating exercise that gets the heart rate up to individual need and keeps it there for at least 20 minutes a day is proper exercise. Of course, if you have particular medical problems, consult your doctor as to the best exercise program for your specific needs. But generally, this is the basic formula to follow:

"Your goal should be to get the heart rate up to 85 percent of the maximum rate for the heart, which is 220 beats per minute. Take 220 and subtract your age. That answer should be multiplied by a percentage that corresponds with your present physical condition and activity level. Sixty (60) percent is suggested to start for those who lead a very sedentary life, all the way up to 80-85 percent for those who are physically active and engage in regular exercise. The answer you receive then is your personal stress rate. You should find an exercise that will take your pulse to that level and maintain it for 20 minutes. To check the exercise, take your pulse after two minutes of swimming, jogging, trampoline, whatever you choose. Take the pulse for 15 seconds and multiply times four (4). This will give you your pulse per minute after two minutes of exercise. The ultimate goal is 85% of your maximum heart rate. For example:

$$
\begin{array}{rl}
220 & \text{(maximum stress rate for heart)} \\
- \ 30 & \text{(your age)} \\
\hline
190 & \\
\times \ .75 & \text{(you are fairly active)} \\
\hline
142.50 & \text{(beats per minute)}
\end{array}
$$

142-143 is then your target. If you take your pulse (after two minutes of running) for 15 seconds and it is 30, then times 4 it is 120. You then know to increase the pace you run. After you reach your target levels, re-evaluate your progress and change targets." (James L. Hodgson, Ph.D., Associate Professor Physiology, Penn State University, *Healthways*, April 1979, p. 6)

The key to effective exercise is not what kind of exercise you do, whether it is swimming, jogging, tennis, track, situps, etc., but which exercise or exercise program is best suited for you. And don't forget self-discipline. No use choosing jogging as your means of exercise if you live in a climate that prevents much outdoor activity, and would mean you would have to drive to a gym and you rarely have a car available to you. Choose an exercise program that you can fit to your present daily routine.

A young mother with four small children decided to try jogging. She had to get up at 4:00 a.m. in order to be back "on duty" before all were awake. She found this not working for her because often the weather was not conducive at that hour. Then she tried jogging around the playpen. Do you know how many times around a playpen you must run in order to go a mile? She got dizzy and decided jogging was not the answer. As she played with her young children, she realized that all their energy in jumping, tumbling, and scrambling was good exercise. She bought some children's exercise records and together, mother and her four little ones discovered a fun activity that enabled her to accomplish this commandment: "And gave unto him commandments which *inspired* him; (D & C 20:7)

3. *Proper Clothing.* You need not "have money" to dress properly or in a manner becoming to you. There are a few basic rules to follow in always looking neat and well-attired:

a. *Be basic:* Start with a skirt, jacket, and pair of slacks that all match in a basic solid color, as neutral as possible. Then add a basic dress in a complementary color. Example: beige jacket, slacks, or skirt can be worn with separate blouses with or without a jacket. A chocolate brown dress can be worn alone for daytime or with beige pearls and beige jacket for dressier occasions. After the basic, you can add other basics. A lot of skirts and slacks in other colors would complement the beige jacket. There are a lot of books, magazines, etc., that can aid you in developing a basic wardrobe. After you establish that, you can then add to and supplement your wardrobe as time goes on.

b. *Simplicity:* Most women are flattered by the more simple and tailored lines. Example: A large neck isn't flattered by ruffles or a fussy neckline. When in doubt, stay simple in style.

c. *Color:* Usually color falls into four groups: Summer (fair-skinned, usually blondes); Spring (ruddier and more pink complexion); Autumn (olive and sallow-skinned); and Winter (very white skin with usually dark hair and eyes). Know what colors best suit you and flatter your skin. Stay with them!

d. *Fit:* Wear clothes that fit. If it's too big or too small, either alter, sell, or give away. There is nothing more unattractive than to see a woman whose bulges are really bulging under skin-tight clothes. Even a slender woman is less attractive in a garment that hugs her body than one which gracefully "flows" over and around her.

The general rule is that "softer" lines make you appear taller, thinner, and more elegant. (That doesn't mean long, flowing housedress with large flowers!) Tip for pregnant women: Choose styles where the shirring begins at neck or shoulders, *never* under the bust line.

    e. *Prints:* Be careful. The old falsehood that large girls can't wear large prints is gone. But choose wisely. Anything that is loud, garish, faddy, or even slightly questionable should be avoided. Many great prints created by great designers are cheaply reproduced on fabrics not suited to that particular design and coloring. Silk takes dyes beautifully and can produce great color effects, but unless you can afford silk prints, don't buy the copies in rayon; they never reproduce the same.

    Above all, avoid the "cutesy," babyish prints that look darling on daughter. You are not a daughter, you are Woman. A lovely, elegant, feminine *Woman!*

    f. *Your body:* Be aware of your physical assets and liabilities. Study your shape and stature and observe styles. Realize that if you have short legs, those great blouson pants that hug at the ankles are not for you. You will have to wear pants, dresses, and skirts that always give you a longer-leg look. We could go on to a whole book here, for as many shapes, sizes, and angles women come in. Play up your good features and use the not-so-good ones to their best advantage. It takes study and trial and error. No one said it would be easy; it just takes self-discipline to spend some time looking at the physical you, and deciding to make the most of you.

    One final note. Stop covering up in those long dresses and don't believe you have to dress like a "frump" to be humble. The warnings are there about costly apparel, and the pride and vanity of worldly things. Let's not confuse the two. How do you think your Father in Heaven dresses? Do you think he wears anything but the finest of cloth and quality? He is perfection — not pride or vanity — but wonderful perfection.

    g. *Research:* Spend the time you need to learn what looks good on you within your budget. The most elegantly-dressed woman I know does not have a lot of clothes. But she has studied her body and has ruled out all that doesn't look good on her. She focuses on all those styles that do. She wears only her "colors" (winter) and keeps her outfits simple and tailored.

4. *Cleanliness.* Never be caught with a head of greasy, dirty hair. Yes, even at home. Your hair is so obvious to you and everyone else. Keep it clean. Toothpaste, deodorant, and shampoo are daily items as essential as food and water. Use them as often as necessary, depending on the climate and your body.

Clothing should ALWAYS be clean, fresh, and pressed.

5. *Accessories.* Decorative items should complement the outfit, not detract. Softness, subtleness, that is the secret. A pair of simple earrings are more flattering to the features than gaudy ones which dangle to the neck or send a message in neon! Earrings are meant to add "sparkle" to the face, not bring attention to the ear.

Necklaces should flatter the neckline and style of the dress. If you have a short, fat neck, you wouldn't want to wear a choker. If your dress has a busy print, you wouldn't want to wear an elaborate necklace. Be choosy. Be meticulous.

Purses and shoes should blend with, not detract, from an outfit. Sometimes shoes look like the main purchase and the outfit, an afterthought.

Scarves and other accessories are meant to enhance the outfit or a person's features. Do not choose that which detracts.

Rule: If all you see is the accessory, it's the wrong choice.

6. *Makeup and Hair.* A famous makeup and hair stylist once said, "I can tell what year a woman graduated from high school by her makeup and hair."

President McKay was reported to have said when asked by the Brethren if the women of the Church should wear makeup, "Well, even an old barn looks better when it's painted."

Here are a few guidelines:

a. If the hair style or makeup is all you see, you've overdone it.

b. Hair should ALWAYS be clean and groomed.

c. Makeup should blend on the face, never make "lines" where the shadow, blush, or foundation "ends."

d. Eyebrows should be kept IMMACULATELY plucked and shaped.

e. *Always* wear mascara and lipstick (no lipstick makes dead lips).

f. *Turquoise* eyeshadow is used for highlighting only. Use only soft shades and highlight with the bright ones.

g. Get a decent haircut, not a do-it-yourselfer. (Choose a hairdresser that you know gives a good cut and has expertise in helping you choose a flattering style.)

Once a year I attend a free makeup demonstration at a local department store. Every cosmetic company sends cosmetologists to various stores throughout the year to demonstrate and sell their product. You can have your makeup done by an expert at no charge. It's a wonderful way to learn what looks good on you among the latest techniques.

It is not possible in this book to give more than a few guidelines in better grooming. The rest is up to you. Go to the library, browse through books and magazines on fashion and makeup. Learn to make wise choices for yourself, not to accept what looks good on others.

Above all, strive to be feminine and simple. Simple does not mean PLAIN. Simple means elegant, not gaudy, overdone, or flashy. Simple means making your appearance show off you, the person.

If this next part of the book doesn't apply to you, read it to help someone else.

Under this category, we should discuss another aspect of physical improvement — the home. Over the years of helping people make their homes a beautiful and functional place to live, I have gained a greater insight into the importance of a well-planned environment in which to live. Now I am not speaking so much of material acquisitions like fine furnishings and accessories, as I am of three other disciplines. They are privacy, personality, and cleanliness. These are three requisites to better physical harmony and self-esteem.

Everyone needs privacy at some point during a day. A home should be planned so that there is a place, even if it is just a chair, where a person can go and not be disturbed. It is necessary to take time to renew and regroup and refuel. This is all discussed in the next chapter, but needs mention her because a home should offer an area of privacy to each family member. Maybe there isn't room for each member to call his or her own, but when a corner is designated for one person, the rest of the family should understand that he or she needs privacy there.

Personality means YOU, the woman of the house. Professionally, I don't believe that old adage, "A man's home is his castle." It's a woman's castle. She cooks in it, cleans it, entertains there, raises her children in it, and lives by its routine. It should reflect HER personality.

I once had some clients where the husband made all the choices. He loved brown, beige, and black, and he had decorated the home with all shades of these colors. I came into the picture because the master bedroom wasn't done yet, and the wife was putting up some resistance. In exasperation, she had said, "If you do our bedroom in brown and black, I won't sleep there!" They came to me to settle the feud. After the first meeting, it was apparent he wanted me to side with him and had expected me to do so. I remained neutral on that first interview. The next day, the wife called me, and in tears said she hated her home. "I'm here all day long and by the end of the day, these colors have made me so nervous I'm a bear with the children. And it's not just that I hate the colors. Have you ever tried to vacuum crackers and crumbs out of chocolate brown carpet? This house is impossible to keep clean. And now he wants a brown and black bedroom. There will be no place where I can escape."

I tried to console her and told her I would do my best to help her. A week later, they came back to my office for a presentation. It was a tense situation. The wife was very quiet.

I began to present the plan. Her favorite colors came first: soft yellows, soft apricots, a touch of raspberry, and lots of creamy white. Then came the fabrics and prints: a small delicate floral, a feminine check, polished cottons and ecru lace. Next I presented the furniture: a soft creamy white finish, country French lines, a chaise made for a lady, and a chair made for a man.

Her apprehension had been overcome, and she seemed to be entranced at the sparkle that lay before them, although she remained reticent. He was obviously petulant. But before either could speak — as they both squirmed, each for their own reason — I said, "Of all the rooms in a home, the master bedroom should be the most feminine. In a feminine room, a woman feels more frilly and soft; she feels more of a woman. And in that same environment, a man feels more masculine, more protective to the dainty lady there. He feels more of a man." To her surprise, he was totally receptive to that idea; it had never before occurred to him. I went on to answer their questions, reassuring them the room would not be *fragile*, only feminine. I got the designing job.

About two months after the work was completed, they came in to see me. There sat in my office a changed couple! He could not believe how much difference the expression of her personality had made in their home. Now he wanted to make some changes in the rest of the home.

Your home should not exclude your husband, but it should be the reflection of you. Even if you lived in a cardboard box, that box should be painted your favorite colors. Your touches, your handiwork, your treasures should be reflected in all parts of your home. It doesn't take money to do that, it takes only you. When all who live around you see your personality, you will have greater feelings of security and confidence. It is also the greatest place to express your talents and interests.

Last of the three, but not least, is cleanliness. If all you had to wear was filthy rags, how soon before your spirits become languid? You cannot live in a dirty or cluttered house and work and perform to full capacity.

The first excuse is that "what's the use of cleaning or repairing, all it is is old, shabby, used furniture and a cheap apartment or trailer or house?" Is that what you see? Here is a favorite little rhyme of mine:

> "Two men looked out from prison bars
> One saw the mud, one saw the stars."

I have, in my lifetime, lived with old, shabby, used furniture in a cheap dwelling. With a few pieces of sandpaper, cans of paint, inexpensive fabric, my little home was transformed from dull into divine! And when the house sparkled, so did I. No one needs to live with worn and dirty things. Even in the mouth of poverty, a good detergent is affordable.

When a home looks clean, smells clean, and is clean, the Spirit of the Lord is easier to invite. The first obvious benefit from cleanliness is freedom from guilt that it is dirty. The second benefit is that your family is learning good techniques and skills from you. The third benefit is that you develop pride in your home and in yourself and have a greater desire to express more of your talents there. The fourth benefit is that others can enjoy your home more. The fifth benefit is that the Savior can come there anytime; you are ready for Him.

When your home is dirty, cluttered, and emits an offensive odor, it reflects the way you feel about yourself. And the physical environment in which you live affects your daily motivation and energy. Apathy breeds apathy.

Busy schedules don't leave much time to shift clutter each day. It's not the clutter of a day of which I'm speaking. It's the honest-to-goodness fungus growing layers everywhere. Toilets, refrigerators, floors, baseboards, draperies, cabinets that have that "help me" look!

When a friend of mine was in the Relief Society presidency, she organized a "houseaholics" group for women in her ward who needed to become better housekeepers. She said the cases were from those who needed matches and gasoline to those who just wanted to improve their homemaking skills. They met every two weeks and learned techniques. It was done by the buddy system. The sisters picked partners, and for each two weeks, would help each other either by phone or physically. The partners would set goals together for the two-week period, and see that they kept each other working. Each session lasted six weeks, and the results were outstanding! I do believe that ward must have put Mr. Clean to shame!

The objective is a clean and fresh place to live in so that you might perform to capacity and feel good about yourself. Cleanliness is next to Godliness. And as for tired, shabby, and worn possessions? They can take on a whole new look with just a little fixing up. Fresh paint on walls brightens a whole room, and clean, crisp draperies add warmth and cheerfulness. A green plant strategically placed says, "I care." A whole new spirit pervades when you begin to look out and see the stars.

Chapter  Four

Develop Your Identity — Socially

Perhaps one of the most dramatic cases of a woman developing herself socially was that of the late Helen Keller. Under great physical handicap she overcame her inadequacies and was able to reach out and touch and help and inspire the lives of countless people. Most women don't have such adverse handicaps and yet, social development is very trying for them.

Do you often feel ill at ease when in a new situation?

Are you uncomfortable when attention is drawn to you?

Have you been at a loss for words when introduced to a stranger?

In a group situation, do you often find yourself talking and "clinging" only to those people you know?

When you have to prepare a lesson, a talk, or participate in a church function, does your whole house fall apart?

When conversations turn toward topics you are unfamiliar with, do you fade away?

When approached with questions about the gospel by non-members, do you lack self-confidence in your answers?

In a Sunday School class, do you fear being called upon to answer a question?

Do you have a difficult time handling a compliment?

Does it unnerve you to speak or pray in a meeting?

Do you apologize before giving a talk or lesson or when stating your opinion?

If you answered yes even to one of the above questions, you have room for social improvement.

1. *Self-Confidence.*   This is achieved through a series of short-term successes. *Competence creates confidence.*

Yes, we've all met Sister Superwoman who bakes all her own bread, sews the family's entire wardrobe (even her bedding, you are told!), wins first place in every fair with her great crafts, looks like she stepped off the cover of Vogue, has her Christmas gifts (all handmade) finished by October, teaches Spiritual living, earns $1,200 a month selling cosmetics out of the trunk of her car, has five well-groomed and well-behaved children, is an attentive wife, and oh, yes, is five months pregnant with number six.

Do you hate her or join her? Well, hate is out of the question. It just isn't the Christian thing to do. But join her? It's too overwhelming. So where do you fall? Somewhere in between modicum of mediocrity and frozen in frustration? Are you involved in every project, every craft, every lesson, every idea that comes along, doing them all "gracefully" but not one thing "greatly"?

How did Sister Superwoman get to where she is? By diving in and spreading herself so thin she never accomplished one project or task to the point of "pure perfection" — but instead, just dabbled here and there? No, that Sister caught the vision of "line upon line, precept upon precept, here a little, there a little; and blessed are those who hearken unto my precepts, and lend an ear unto my counsel, for they shall learn wisdom; for *unto him that receiveth I will give more.*" (2 Nephi 28:30)

And in the *Doctrine and Covenants* we read " that every man may improve upon his talent; that every man may gain other talents, yea, even an hundred fold. . ." (Section 82:18)

In every facet of earthly existence — which centers around self-improvement and perfection — the counsel of the Lord applies.

Remember, self-confidence is achieved through a series of short-term successes. These are goals which you can accomplish quickly and without overwhelming obstacles. When making short-term goals, never challenge yourself with what may be extremely difficult for you to achieve at your present level and should be categorized as a long-range goal.

Examples:

Long-range goal	Celestial kingdom
Short-range goal	Pay full tithing
	Obey word of wisdom
	Be honest
	Pray often
Long-range goal	Perfection in a talent
Short-range goal	Take lessons
	Practice four hours a day
	Give a recital
	Teach others

Sometimes goals need to be changed after they have been established. Priorities change, and the need arises to alter the goal. Ten years ago, I had four goals that seemed important to me. I said that before life was over, I desired to fly an airplane, design the interior of a private plane, learn to ski, and ride a horse. I accomplished the first three, and to this day, do not know how to ride a horse. Ten years later, it just isn't important anymore. That goal has been replaced with what, to me, are more substantial and creative goals. As self-esteem develops, so do more meaningful priorities. Replacing goals should not be a self-serving excuse. But replacing goals because of personal development is not an empty rationalization.

Whether your goals are spiritual or temporal, they should be righteously beneficial to you and those involved. If you set a goal that is improbable to achieve and you don't meet the goal in the time allotted, your confidence weakens. Then what benefit has that goal been? None.

Start with simple goals for immediate achievement. Then add more difficult ones, always keeping in mind the long-range ones. Little by little you will achieve, excel, and gain confidence.

Remember, *competence creates confidence.* When you learn to do something well, within perfection, you gain confidence. Confidence then assures you that you can tackle something else, perhaps even more difficult.

Don't worry about Sister Superwoman being the rule rather than the exception and that you simply don't measure up. You are in competition with only you. Be the BEST that YOU can be. You are bound to make mistakes and fail. Failure can be overcome. It is the fear of failure that impedes progress and confidence.

Shakespeare said· "Present fears are less than horrible imaginings."

Is it possible to attain perfection in mortal life? Yes, in many areas, although the perfecting process goes on into the next life, until we become perfect in Jesus Christ.

To look at perfection in a total sense is overwhelming. The Lord intended us to endeavor, to work, to endure to the end, to *strive* for perfection. You can become perfect in paying tithing, temple attendance, patience, word of wisdom, speaking kindly, and on and on. You can take a talent and concentrate on it and practice it until you perfect it to the epitome of its nature. The urgent concern here is that you realize *it is not WHAT you do, but HOW you do it!*

For years, I have seen the women underdeveloped in their specific areas of talents and accomplishments. They seem to want to do it all — instead of searching for those few things that are especially familiar to them, and working toward perfection within their range.

It is not WHERE you serve the Lord, but HOW you serve Him! You cannot compare your talents, callings, or circumstances with anyone else. Your confidence will come only through your personal achievement. It has been said *if you can't be a success being yourself, you can't be it by being someone else.*

2. *Dealing with Guilt.* A beloved friend of mine wrote:

> *I discovered, just after I was married, an attitude that is of epidemic proportion among Latter-day Saint women and cripples their self-esteem strides instantly. There is a pervading emotional dishonesty! The dishonesty is created by guilt which never surfaces to be dealt with; rather smoulders beneath the surface, robbing and caustically eating at self-esteem.*

The seeds of this dishonesty lie in the inability to deal with the ideal when the present does not conform. As Latter-day Saints, our goals are so lofty, so high, a woman feels failure if she can't "do it all." She is unable to accept the fact that she hasn't reached the ideal and doesn't measure up.

My friend went on to say:

> *I was 27 when my first child was born. I had lived a lifestyle that seemed externally controllable. But when that little person came, I had to learn to cope when someone else was in control — or seemed to be. I, at that point, was hit with the forceful concept that all we can control is ourselves and influence is the only effect we can have on others. I've known women literally getting headaches in Church because they were trying to control something at best they could only influence. Influence is a friend type of concern, stemming from love. Control creates tension and destroys tenderness. There were several times during this first year of motherhood when I reminded the Lord in my prayers of my address because I had never run so hard on so little rest. I wasn't depressed, just confused on how to mold all my responsibilities around this child. There are some critical balances which must be solved by each woman at this point. How can you preserve your individuality and self-expression? How do you create time for yourself and not feel guilty? How do you resolve the peer pressure of what you should do to be a 'good' mother? What alterations must you make in your lifestyle to maintain sanity? The 'answers' to these questions are not as important as 'who' makes the decision. If you, after consultation with*

your husband and the Lord, make them, the results will nurture self-esteem and bring buoyancy into your life. If your husband, mother, mother-in-law, or friends, etc., make your choices, you know the results.

Maybe all your decisions are not going to be correct, but you will become more confident as YOU stand in the light of your own thoughts and honesty.

I never wanted to nurse my children. Pregnancy was a hardship for me — a nine-month flu. When it was over, I wanted it to be OVER. My biggest problem in dealing with it was the guilt inflicted upon me by well-meaning friends and loved ones. Everyone was certain I could not be a good mother, and the children would develop an unknown disease if I did not nurse! Even up to the hour of delivery, pressure came from the nurses, and it was hard for me to cough out "not nursing." Weeks afterwards, as I cuddled and hugged my bottle-fed baby, no desire to nurse had been kindled but plenty of guilt. And then came the dawn. It was MY decision, and it was RIGHT for ME. My mother or mother-in-law or husband didn't have to nurse that baby, so they couldn't make that decision. From that moment on, as I accepted the responsibility of the decision, I was free, and the guilt was gone, "baby and mother doing well." (And I am happy to report after three children, not one has contracted that unknown disease!)

Now, I am not advocating that women should not nurse their children. What I am trying to point out is that a woman should be responsible for her OWN decisions. She is the one who has to live with the choices. No one else can make those choices for her if she is to be happy.

My sister told me of an incident when she was just plain tired of changing messy pants. With two in diapers and one being potty-trained, she had had enough this particular day. When her husband came home, she asked him to please change mess number twelve for the day. He said, "Oh, honey, I hate it, why don't you?" She said, "Oh, honey, because I hate it, too!" And he said, "Oh, you can't because you're the mother. . ." (I won't finish the story; he really is a loving husband and father, and we've all forgiven him!)

Whether spoken or not, women are made to feel they have to LOVE everything they are supposed to do. That is just not the truth.

And when you begin to feel a distaste for a task, a flood of guilt pours into your soul, "Oh, I must like this, I am the mother." It's OKAY not to like it. You must love the calling — it's a calling from the Lord — but you don't have to love *all* the duties. But it is important that we learn the law of sacrifice through some of our arduous tasks. Sacrifice is not often pleasant or it wouldn't be a sacrifice. I doubt the Savior physically enjoyed His sacrifice. Sacrifices must be patiently borne. It comes slowly. You must be honest with yourself and don't try to hide or repress those feelings of not being able to deal with the ideal. That wasn't the plan. The plan was for you to come to earth and understand:

Life's Plan

Receive Callings

    Single Adult
    Wife
    Mother
    Single Parent

Teach and Learn

    By trial and error
    By obedience to commandments
    By decision-making

Growth in Strength

   Through problems and trials
   Through blessings
   Through talents
   Through sacrifices

Return Home

   With more than with what you left.

When you harbor guilt for not "measuring up," you aren't following the plan, or you are letting Satan get the best of you.

What does that mean, "not measuring up"? Does that mean not fitting into the MOLD? It is said by some there are those who just don't seem to fit into the mold of a typical Mormon woman. What does that mean? Does that really infer they are different because they work, don't have six children, or seem to shine way out in front of others because of achievement?

What is THE MOLD? Are you of THE MOLD? Do you harbor guilt feelings because you don't think you measure up to THE MOLD?

Let's dispell this mold myth right now! It's moldy! *The mold image is a lack of self-image, a lack of personal identity and self-esteem..* You are what you were like before you came to earth. Your personality is basically the same. For every woman born, there is a different personality. There lies in each woman her own package. Included in that package are weaknesses, desires, strengths, talents, goals, etc., all different from the next woman. There may be some same things in others' packages, but no two are identical. What is good for one is not good for another. What works for one will not work for another. What one desires another does not. To inflict one woman's choices and circumstances on another could destroy that other woman. The "mold" is for those who haven't opened the package yet.

We have certain basics that are God-given and inherent

feminine characteristics such as: maternal instincts, desires to protect and be protected, higher levels of tenderness, compassion, and spirituality, etc. But that's where the similarities end. Then each separate personality takes over. The Church leaders counsel the women collectively because they can't counsel each woman individually. But the counsel is meant to be individual and personal. This is not to say we manipulate the counsel to justify our selfish motives or desires. When the Church leaders counsel to have as many children as possible, it is the "as possible" that becomes personal and individual. It takes into consideration physical and emotional and environmental conditions of the family and mother. There is nowhere in the scriptures where it says you must have "X" number of children to gain the celestial kingdom. The Lord has asked us to multiply and replenish the earth. He has given us intelligence and a heart to understand His desires for us personally.

A friend of mine who has eight children is a well-organized and effective mother. She told me she always wanted and could handle a big family, and she always wanted about five children. As each child was born, she always had the feeling "one more." After number five, the feeling was still there; she counseled with the Lord and knew His desires. With each of the next two, there was the feeling, "one more." Then at the birth of her eighth child, distinctly she felt, "It is enough; these were the ones to be sent to you." The feelings of "one more" stopped, and she is at peace over her decision.

Another friend of mine who has three children is a good mother, also. She is of totally different temperment than the other mother. She expressed the same feelings to me: "one more," until number three child came. Then those feelings were gone. She too is at peace with her decision to stop.

For one it was eight children, for another it was three, both obedient Latter-day Saint women, both good mothers. The same Father in Heaven, the same counsel, but two different women and two different circumstances.

As long as righteous motives and reasons prevail, you are doing what the Lord asks. But ask Him, He will whisper to you. Be sensitive to His spirit. You will know in your heart what is right for you. You will have opened your OWN package.

What about guilt feelings dealing with material things such as money, clothes, cars, makeup, etc.? Is it wrong to desire nice things or want better material circumstances? Absolutely not! To want to achieve and have the good things of the earth is not base or carnal. What kind of home do you think the Father lives in? A mansion, we are told. His clothes are probably the finest of cloth; Joseph Smith saw the streets paved in gold. We decorate our temples with only the most elegant materials.

However, seeking first the Kingdom is a commandment: "But seek ye first the kingdom of God and his righteousness, and all these things shall be added unto you." (3 Nephi 14:33)

It is when the desire for material gain becomes a priority that a hazardous climate exists. It also shows a lack of self-esteem.

It was once important to me to have the right label in my clothes, the right signature bag, and other self-important material things. *As self-esteem develops, it isn't necessary to prove yourself to anyone except yourself.* Most people who flaunt their material possessions in a condescending manner, or seem to have an insatiable quest for more and more, are really suffering from a tremendous lack of self-esteem. They are trying to spell success m-o-n-e-y, when success is spelled s-e-l-f e-s-t-e-e-m.

It's not wrong to want to look pretty or have nice things. It is wrong to overindulge yourself. There is too much suffering in this world to have surplus and not use it to help others. If you are caught up in the pride and vanity of the world, you *should* feel guilty. You must distinguish between wants and needs. If you have three cars and you need three cars, then you are within the bounds of the Lord's law.

And behold, thou wilt remember the poor, and consecrate of thy properties for their support that which thou hast to impart unto them, with a covenant and a deed which cannot be broken.

And inasmuch as ye impart of your substance unto the poor, ye will do it unto me; and they shall be laid before the bishop of my church and his counselors, two of the elders, or high priests, such as he shall appoint or has appointed and set apart for that purpose.

And it shall come to pass, that after they are laid before the bishop of my church, and after that he has received these testimonies concerning the consecration of the properties of my church, that they cannot be taken from the church, agreeable to my commandments, every man shall be made accountable unto me, a steward over his own property, or that which he has received by consecration, as much as is sufficient for himself and family.

And again, if there shall be properties in the hands of the church, or any individuals of it, more than is necessary for their support after this first consecration, which is a residue to be consecrated unto the bishop, it shall be kept to administer to those who have not, from time to time, that every man who has need may be amply supplied and receive according to his wants.

Therefore, the residue shall be kept in my storehouse, to administer to the poor and the needy, as shall be appointed by the high council of the church, and the bishop and his church;

And for the purpose of purchasing lands for the public benefit of the church, and building houses of worship, and building up of the New Jerusalem which is hereafter to be revealed—

That my covenant people may be gathered in one in that day when I shall come to my temple. And this I do for the salvation of my people.

And it shall come to pass, that he that sinneth and repenteth not shall be cast out of the church, and shall not receive again that which he has consecrated unto the poor and the needy of my church, or in other words, unto me—

For inasmuch as ye do it unto the least of these, ye do it unto me.

> For it shall come to pass, that which I spake by the mouths of my prophets shall be fulfilled; for I will consecrate of the riches of those who embrace my gospel among the Gentiles unto the poor of my people who are of the house of Israel.
>
> And again, thou shalt not be proud in thy heart; let all thy garments be plain, and their beauty the beauty of the work of thine own hands; (D & C 42:30-40)

But if you have three expensive cars and you need only one, you may be in danger of violating the law. If you are seeking first the Kingdom of God, your desires are natural and Godlike, and all else will be added unto you. It should be understood, though, that just because a member is affluent, does not mean they are more spiritual, and likewise, if someone is poor, it does not mean they are unrighteous.

When the Church leaders counsel women to stay home and raise their children, again, they are counseling collectively, and again, it is an individual decision. A decision such as that is to be taken to your Father in Heaven. He knows you, and what is truly in your heart.

Some women HAVE to work because they must supplement an income in these days of rising inflation. Some HAVE to work because they are the sole support or single parent. Some HAVE to work because they are born with an insatiable drive and desire to work or create.

Those who are born with this drive don't do it for the money. If they were told tomorrow that they would never receive another dime for what they did, they would still do it. They are BETTER wives and mothers because they DO work. These are the exceptions, not the rule. To put them in another's package would destroy them.

The whole key to peace of mind is what is in the heart and what you have settled with your Father in Heaven. To leave your families for more material luxuries is not a righteous motive. You know it, and the Lord knows it, and you won't feel good about yourself.

A long time ago I let others inflict guilt feelings upon me about working. The sharpest knives came from those who supposedly knew me best. I was even accused of being so shallow as to put my work first and the family and church second.

It came to a point in my life that I had either to give it up or live in mental agony. So I took it to the Lord. As He and I talked it over, a line in my patriarchal blessing came into my mind, the meaning of which became clear. At that moment, I knew in my heart I was developing myself and my talents for further purposes, perhaps known only to the Lord. No matter what others said, I knew that my family and the Church came first. I knew that I could manage that. I knew my capacity to make quality time instead of quantity time. I also knew that being self-employed I could arrange my schedule around my children's school and activities and be home when they were home. For me it was a personal package, mine alone.

But most important of all, I had taken it up with the Lord, and He had whispered to me. I was at peace. He knows each of us. If it is right, you will have peace.

What about you single sisters who must work in order to earn the living? Some of you married sisters must work to help your husbands. Your guilt feelings center around doubts of being able to provide a good gospel training base for the children. There is always a way. Remember QUALITY time, not quantity time. The most important thing to remember is that you must TAKE IT UP WITH THE LORD. Through the inspiration of the Holy Ghost and by earnest supplication on your part, you will be directed as to the best methods and use of your time with your family. You will be able to receive renewed strength and vigor in managing all your duties. And you will be inspired to be sensitive to their wants and needs. (Two good articles on this subject are found in the *Ensign* magazine: March 1980, p. 39 and July 1980, p. 40.)

Some of you sisters think you want to work; some have given

up a career to have children; some don't want to work but feel cheated because you haven't been able to fully develop a talent. Do you feel guilty or have a poor self-image for having such thoughts? DON'T! (Remember, we discarded THE MOLD; you are an individual.)

To want to achieve, excel, and create is Godlike. He placed those feelings in you. Your choice was to raise up the little ones full time. You know in your heart that's where you need to be and want to be. If you had to choose again, you would choose the same. But what do you do about those feelings?

Don't ignore them. They won't go away. Admit them out loud. They are not bad or wicked, but you have to do something about them. So you say, "What can I do? I have four kids, two in diapers, and three loads of wash a day." Or you say, "I am too old now."

You work on those feelings one at a time, and you go to the Lord. You are privileged to the same inspiration from the Holy Ghost. It's a matter of developing a talent and ability until you achieve perfection in at least one thing. There are many who have even turned a talent into a little business without leaving home. I personally know women who teach music or art or needlecraft lessons; those who decorate cakes, do flower arranging for weddings, sell cosmetics, soap, or jewelry; those who cater parties, do calligraphy, sew, teach sewing; those who sell artwork or handicrafts, and so on and so on. They have opened their "packages."

Remember, to desire to achieve, excel, or create is natural and God-given. Don't feel guilty for your feelings. Each has a package of personal capacity. Counsel with the Lord and ask His advice. Sisters, it is my opinion based on all I have read or spiritually felt, that the best and most talented women were SAVED to be born in this the last dispensation of the gospel. The best of all He has. The Spirit of the Lord is with them. It rested on them with the Suffrage Movement, the formation of the Relief Society, the establishment of programs for women at the Brigham Young Academy (now University). His spirit has rested with them, you, on all endeavors in behalf of *excellence and freedom* for women. It is wrong to be repressed or to repress those feelings of excellence and freedom. However, Satan has used these natural underlying currents to his advantage. What women are feeling about being repressed, members and non-members alike, is right. Satan is playing on their feelings and shaping them to his own designs. No, freedom is not leaving behind responsibilities of wifehood, motherhood, charity, and chastity. Freedom is realizing that you have a choice calling from the Father, and that you possess tools (talents) by which to accomplish His work. Freedom is realizing that you can only proceed at full speed when you know how individual and choice you are. Freedom is realizing you were born to do His work and He gave you the talents by which to do it. (See 1 Nephi 3:7.) Throw away the MOLD. Accept the responsibilities for your own choices and have your Heavenly Father help you open your package. It has been wrapped with a beautiful ribbon — His understanding.

3. *Handling Rejection.* This brings us to the second area of focus, handling rejection. Whether it is done directly or indirectly, by friends, associates, workers, or family members, everyone experiences some form of rejection occasionally. DON'T TAKE IT PERSONALLY. Sometimes it's your idea, a thought, an action, even a project. You know when others really don't like it, don't you? It's not you as a person that's being rejected. Others simply have an opinion of what they like or don't like. Don't defend yourself either. The idea is to develop the confidence that you are doing the best you can and are still learning. Accept you for who you are. Very rarely is rejection from others meant personally.

Often feelings of rejection are self-inflicted because of lack of self-esteem. A woman once told me she felt rejected by the more affluent members of her ward because she was poor. I knew the particular people she was referring to, and I knew they didn't feel that way at all. She was feeling inferior because her levels of achievement were low. She set goals but admitted she almost never followed through and accomplished them. She didn't feel good about her talents, her appearance, her responsibilities as a mother, etc. So she blamed much of her misery on rejection from others. It was all self-inflicted. Economic discrimination has no room in the Kingdom of God. Happy, well-adjusted, achieving people are gregarious with one another, no matter what the environment or status from which they come.

Sometimes you think others don't like your personality because you are shy, boring, or have an accent or whatever. These again are feelings of weakness. You are fearing what is only fear. You must reach a little further, breathe a little deeper, and gain courage to accept those feelings as weakness and then go about setting goals to correct them.

Single, divorced, and childless sisters have dual feelings of rejection as they often feel they have also been rejected by the Lord. These become extremely personal and emotional feelings.

Our goals in the Church are centered around the family unit. There is a young woman who has been married for four years and has no children. She confided in me, "If one more person says, 'Why don't you have any kids?' I think I'll tell them it's because I never gave it much thought!" Of course, that's all she thinks about. There is another young woman who has never married, and all she hears is, "Why aren't you married yet?" Finally, once in frustration, she blurted out, "Because nobody's asked me yet!" And then Satan comes along and whispers and antagonizes, "You aren't good enough. You are unworthy. You are being punished." These are all lies. However, others too can make you feel guilty and unworthy, even your own family and friends. Their comments are sometimes well meaning, sometimes not well meaning, and sometimes thoughtless. You find yourself becoming overwhelmed with feelings of guilt, bitterness, misunderstanding, and doubt.

Forgive those around you and realize that the Lord loves you. You are not unworthy and are not being punished. That is just simply not the Lord's way. But His way is a school of trial and testing. It doesn't matter what others may say, but rather, what is in your heart and between you and the Lord. It is a privilege and blessing to be tried and tested. The Lord tries those whom He loves. He wants a proven people, those who will endure to the end.

It is natural to feel rejected — as though you don't belong — when all your friends and family are married and/or have children. Even simple conversation can be stymied by this apparent gap in common bonds. Innocent statements from others become mentally exaggerated by you as offensive remarks. I know of several childless couples who express that they "kind of build a wall up and hide behind it" so that on the outside it appears as if all is under control. Hiding feelings away is not being honest with yourself and is destructive to self-esteem.

How you handle and control the remarks, social pressure, and emotions is completely up to you. You cannot blame others for their thoughtlessness and thus excuse yourself away behind a wall and become a social recluse. You must rise above the inconsiderate words and guilt feelings and demonstrate a positive mental attitude. "I will depend on the Lord's good judgment."

Guilt feelings are self-inflicted. Yes, they can be suggested to you verbally, but what you do with them once you hear them is up to you. My favorite Chinese proverb says, "You can't stop a robin from lighting in your hair, but you CAN keep it from building a nest there." Think of how much work it takes to build a nest, twig by twig, packed with mud, entangled with the surface on which it's built. You can't stop the words from entering your mind, but you can stop whatever happens from then on. If negative and selfish thoughts are allowed to continually build upon one another, fairly soon the nest is built and entangled in your hair. Oh how difficult it is then to remove.

Are not questions like "Why me?" purely selfish? Is ME not the most selfish thought we have?

A young couple with no children stopped asking those questions and started to ask a new question: "Father, how do you want us to serve you?" Asking that question has changed their lives. They still pray for children, but they have learned to have patience and understanding. They can feel the Lord's love for them. They have found: "He that findeth his life shall lose it: and he that loseth his life for my sake, shall find it." (Mosiah 2:17)

This is not a passive life. If we are anxiously engaged in the Lord's work and glory, nothing is taken away from us. The movie Ben Hur is about the Savior. Judah Ben Hur becomes a political prisoner and is sentenced to become a galley slave, which means certain death. He is cruelly marched to his destination over the hot desert sands. The group passes the village Nazareth where all the prisoners are allowed a drink of water to quench their thirst, except for Ben Hur. The Savior, working as a carpenter before His mission, witnesses the action and gives Ben Hur a dipper of cool water. As the story progresses, Ben Hur saves the life of his captain, and through heroic acts, becomes a free man. On the agonizing death walk to Calvary, he has the opportunity to give the Savior a dipper of cool water, a chance to express his gratitude for the Savior's kindness to him.

The Savior has given us all a dipper of water. He has quenched our thirst for eternal life. Every time we give a dipper of water to the thirsty, we are giving it to the Savior. "Inasmuch as ye have done it unto one of the least of these my brethren, ye have done it unto me." (Matthew 25:40)

It is dangerous to let the robin build a nest of self-pity, despair, self-serving thoughts or desires. It can only lead from the door of light towards the door of darkness. It will only accentuate a lack of self-esteem, a lack of self-worth, because of seemingly not conforming to the mold or ideal. Because some of you may not have all the blessings which you desire at this time, that does not mean a part of yours have been "taken away." It is a mistake for women to believe that life only begins with marriage or children. A woman can have and must have an identity and useful life with or without children or marriage. There can be an "adding to" your person. Turn your life and thoughts to helping others. Other benefits will ensue, such as a wonderful self-esteem, a freedom from the shackles of self-pity, loneliness, and discouragement. You will lift others and, in turn, be lifted yourself.

> They that wait upon the Lord shall renew their strength; they shall mount up with wings as eagles; they shall run and not be weary; and they shall walk and not faint. (Isaiah 40:31)

Sisters, go out and SOAR LIKE AN EAGLE!

4. *Organize.* Organize yourself and your thoughts. You cannot accomplish many things, even one goal to perfection, unless you are organized. Time, money, thoughts, and resources must be organized efficiently. For example:

> You are the Spiritual Living Teacher for your ward Relief Society. Your current lesson is on the 89th Section of the *Doctrine and Covenants*. Also, this month you must make two birthday dresses for twin nieces, do visiting teaching, attend a temple session to which you are committed, and you've been asked to substitute your daughter's primary class next week. Is your whole family going to notice a Nervous Nellie? Is there going to be an upset to your regular lifestyle? Is your regular lifestyle already upset? What will the morning of your lesson be like at home? A scene of preparation, or a scene of anxiety and urgency?

Busy Latter-day Saint women MUST have somewhat of a

living/working schedule if they are to accomplish all they must do in these hectic, harried days. For some it needs to be more rigid than others. Some may desire more flexibility, depending on lifestyles. But the ONLY WAY you can allow time for everything you want and must do is to organize time, money, thoughts, and resources.

Time is number one because once you do that, you'll have opportunity to do the others.

A basic schedule is nothing more than saying Monday — wash day, Tuesday — civic or community work, Wednesday — preparing menus and marketing, Thursday — cleaning house, Friday — church work (visiting teaching, preparing lessons, etc.), Saturday — spending time with the family and preparing for the Sabbath, and Sunday — for family home evening and genealogy. Use whatever schedule works for you. A more concise schedule could break up the days into morning, afternoon, evening, and even more organized, by groups of hours. Weeks should be organized Sabbath to Sabbath so that you can get a perspective of the whole week and plan priorities.

> Organize yourselves; prepare every needful thing; and establish a house, even a house of prayer, a house of fasting, a house of faith, a house of learning, a house of glory, a house of order, a house of God; (D & C 88:119)

In organizing time, remember some guidelines:

a. *Be flexible for that unexpected event:* A last-minute assignment, emergency, promptings from the spirit, the needs of a child or someone else, a chance to teach the gospel. Being flexible doesn't mean finding excuses not to do the task. You must adhere to the schedule as planned when you can do so.

b. *The schedule is to serve you, not you to serve the schedule.* If you are so rigid you must do such and such at an exact time, you may miss out on wonderful experiences that are only for the moment. Also, change it as need arises.

c. *Practice self-discipline:*

> Therefore, cease from all your light speeches, from all laughter, from all your lustful desires, from all your pride and light-mindedness, and from all your wicked doings. (D & C 88:121)

5. *Continue to Increase Your Knowledge.* As you make goals and achieve them, you must immediately replace them with new ones, never ending. You must read all the standard works and then reread them, and then again, never ending. If talking to people is a problem, read books like *How to Win Friends and Influence People,* and other related books. Take lessons in your areas of talent. As you increase your knowledge, doors will open and self-confidence will strengthen. You will be amazed at what powers your mind has. And you will love what you have learned, and you will love you.

> And as all have not faith, seek ye diligently and teach one another words of wisdom; yea, seek ye out of the best books words of wisdom; seek learning, even by study and also by faith. (D & C 88:118)

Certain people just seem to make you feel comfortable when they're around. You spend a few minutes with them and feel as if you've known them half your life. How is it done?

Here are eight steps that will help you put people at ease, make yourself feel secure, and turn acquaintances into instant friends:

1. *Ask Questions.* Almost anyone will answer a question, no matter how shy they are. Start with a question that is personal but innocuous. Barbara Walters got a long and wonderful interview with Aristotle Onassis by asking him about his first job. A prominent woman executive says she always asks people what they did that morning. It's a banal question, but it gets things going. From there you can

move on to other matters, sometimes even more personal. People love to talk about themselves.

2. *Really Listen.* This seems obvious, but making people feel comfortable isn't simply a matter of making idle conversation. You are really asking, "What sort of person are you?" *Really* listening does not mean changing the subject. If someone sticks to a topic, he or she is really interested in it.

Really listening means listening not just to words but tones of voice. I once called a client and as we talked over the phone, in her *tone* of voice I could tell she was in turmoil, even though we were only discussing wallpaper. When I asked if everything was okay, she was surprised at my really "listening," and she broke down; she needed desperately to talk to someone. Really listening means with your eyes, too. Look attentive; don't let your gaze wander. They think they are boring you.

3. *Laugh.* Laughter is warming and friendly. Don't be afraid to laugh or laugh at yourself. Humor is always a common denominator.

Elder Paul H. Dunn tells this story of when he was in the Army in World War II. He was always trying to find the right moment and the privacy to pray in a barrack with 50 men on the floor. He would try to get the end bunk, and wait until all the lights would go out before crawling out of bed to pray. One night, after lights were out and he was on his knees praying, two "half-stewed" men came in, flipped on the lights, and woke everyone up. All saw him on his knees.

"One of them, pointing to me, shouted so all could hear, 'Hey, Holy Paul, pray for me!' I felt a little chagrined and somewhat embarrassed, and I thought to myself, 'Now what do you do?' My mother taught me a great principle. She used to say, 'In delicate situations, use a sense of humor; it always helps.' So while still on my knees, I squared my shoulders, looked at both of the soldiers, and said, 'would you give me your full names because I don't think the Lord knows you.' "

4. *Touch People Occasionally.* Don't overdo it, but touches are supportive and reassuring, a way to say "you're right" without using words. Your own judgment will be your guide. If a person withdraws, you've overdone it. Just a little touch on the shoulder or hand or arm is enough.

5. *Be Helpful and Thoughtful.* If in the conversation you can recommend a new hairdresser, cleaners, toothpaste, or restaurant, do it and write it down on a piece of paper. He or she will probably keep that piece of paper around for a long time and remember you and your thoughtfulness.

6. *Do Not Be Afraid To Say I Like You.* You'd be surprised how many old friends have never said, "I like you," or "I love you" to each other. When was the last time you said it to someone other than your family? When was the last time you said it to yourself? It's important to tell yourself "I love you." It's a commandment: *"Love* (thy neighbor as) *Thyself."*

People so seldom express their feelings toward one another that you can have a tremendous influence by doing it. If there is something you like about a person, tell them. Don't think it, say it. You'll be building your own confidence and their confidence, too.

Sometimes when I've said "I like you," or "I love you," I've met with startled reaction, but never negative and always a reaction that warms the relationship. I hardly knew this young woman who brought me a loaf of bread and admitted she had felt negative feelings towards me. But I told her "I love you," and I meant it. The veil was withdrawn and we discovered a friendship that existed in the eternities. Now words cannot express the love that is shared between us.

7. *Establish A Quick Alliance.* Making people feel comfortable with an attitude, a way of looking at life. We are all together. We are all in the same stream or plan. This has got to be a genuine feeling, sincere feeling.

8. *Cement A Parting.* Offer a good handshake, with a good smile, eye-to-eye contact, maybe even a second extra handsqueeze. To those you are very close to, give a hug.

But it's not all done with body language. If you've enjoyed being with someone, if you want to see that person again, don't keep it a secret. Let people know how you feel, sincerely, and they'll walk away feeling as if they have known you half their life.

"For all have not every gift given unto them; for there are many gifts, and to every man is given a gift...." (D & C 46:11)

EVERYONE is given at least one talent. But that is not enough. We are under solemn obligation as daughters of God to develop our talents to the fullest degree within our mental and physical power.

But how do you find or determine what talent or talents you have? It's easy; just pay attention. Is there something you do or say that causes others to compliment you often? Do you notice those same compliments over and over? (I love your smile; you do such a good job teaching the five-year olds; your hair always looks so nice; etc.) Is there something that you say or do that seems to come easy to you? (Giving a talk, baking bread, sewing, etc.) Is there something you say or do that, although you don't actively pursue it, seems familiar to you? (Poetry, painting, fixing up your home, counseling others.)

You discover your talents by paying attention. Age has nothing to do with it; any age can produce a new talent.

A woman once told me she thought she had no talents. It shocked me. She was a good artist and had mastered calligraphy, in addition to many homemaking skills. She did not consider these talents because she had never given them thought in that scope. They had become second nature, and she had only done them for her own entertainment.

I had the same experience. I just did tasks as they came along; it was part of me. I never really considered them talents, just part of my industrious life and work. As others began to point out my talents, I had to stop and think, "Yes, these are special gifts." Once recognized as such, I was better able to concentrate efforts to develop them and even recognize other ones.

Your talents have been given to you for wise purposes known by the Lord. "To some is given one, and to some is given another, that all may be profited thereby." (D & C 46:12)

In order for you to profit by these, and also for others to profit from your talents, you must be earnestly seeking to *find* them and *develop* them.

There is a little fairy tale written by Og Mandino about a boy who captures a star with a kite. The star's name is Acabar, and he teaches the boy that heavenly secrets are to be found right here on earth. Here is what he says about talents:

> Along with the power of choice you received the most precious gift our Creator can bestow: The spark of life. With it came an obligation to apply your own special talents, whatever they may be, to leave this world a better place than you found it. Billions of humans have failed in this obligation and wasted their lives. (Og Mandino, *The Gift of Acabar,* p. 58)

Let's add one more thing: To leave this earth a *better person* than when you came.

It doesn't matter if you have only ONE and it seems as if others have multiple talents. Study, learn, practice, and develop that talent until you become proficient, confident, and master of it. An amazing process will begin to unfold. The mastery of one talent opens doors to others.

This is a true story of how a talent can develop:

You like to hear poetry (it's comfortable to your ears, seems familiar).

You enjoy reading it.

You read it aloud to others.

You seem to develop a style of reading it that others enjoy; you are asked to read it often.

You find yourself thinking poetic thoughts.

You use poetic phrases.

You begin to express your feelings in poetic style.

You being to write poetry.

You take classes and study poetry.

You write more fluent poetry (and now prose).

Your poetry is enjoyed by others.

You write poetry for others.

You teach a class.

You begin to write lyrics for music.

You are asked to sing your lyrics.

You are asked to sing with other groups.

You find a love and enjoyment in singing. (It is familiar to you.)

Through lessons and practice, you develop that singing ability and receive recognition for it.

You are asked to write poems and songs for special events and programs; you try to print with the pen in an attractive style.

You begin to practice calligraphy.

You take lessons in calligraphy.

Soon you are being asked to hand-letter posters, programs, special messages.

As you become familiar with a drawing tool, you experiment with sketching.

You find a "knack" for sketching and drawing.

You take lessons and practice, and soon you are really drawing.

Your artwork becomes recognized.

This woman, a sister from Utah, who thought she had NO talent has developed an ability to write poetry and prose, sing, do calligraphy, and draw. This is because she paid attention to what felt familiar to her. She was simply re-learning what she already knew.

Developing a talent is increasing your knowledge. It is discovering those special gifts that are for your profit. Do not be threatened by others' gifts, but be eager and willing to learn from them. Know that as you are faithful in developing one talent, the Lord will bless you with others, ". . .that every man may improve upon his talent, that every man may gain other talents. . . ." (D & C 82:18)

Above all, be honest with yourself and others about your talents. Do not profess humility by saying you have no talent, when in your heart you know you do. It is not wrong to say, "I have a talent in doing this and such." It will help you to strengthen your attitude toward that talent, and help others recognize it. Perhaps people will call on you for your help, and their invitation will be an open commitment to keep those talents polished and shining brightly!

6. *Take Time for Self!* Carol Lynn Pearson has written a poem called "Millie's Mother's Red Dress":

It hung there in the closet
While she was dying, Mother's red dress,
Like a gash in the row
Of dark, old clothes
She had worn away her life in.

They had called me home,
And I knew when I saw her
She wasn't going to last.

When I saw the dress, I said,
"Why Mother — how beautiful!
I've never seen it on you."

"I've never worn it," she slowly said.
"Sit down, Millie — I'd like to undo
A lesson or two before I go, if I can."

I sat by her bed.
And she sighed a bigger breath
Than I thought she could hold.
"Now that I'll soon be gone,
I can see some things.
Oh, I taught you good — but I taught you wrong."

"What do you mean, Mother?"

"Well — I always thought
That a good woman never takes her turn,
That she's just for doing for somebody else.
Do here, do there, always keep
Everybody else's wants tended and make sure
Yours are at the bottom of the heap.

Maybe someday you'll get to them,
But of course you never do.
My life was like that — doing for your dad,
Doing for the boys, for your sisters, for you."

"You did — everything a mother could."

"Oh, Millie, Millie, it was no good—
For you — for him. Don't you see?
I did you the worst of wrongs.
I asked nothing — for me!

"Your father in the other room,
All stirred up and staring at the walls—
When the doctor told him, he took
It bad — came to my bed and all but shook
The life right out of me. 'You can't die,
Do you hear? What'll become of me?
What'll become of me?'
It'll be hard, all right, when I go.
He can't even find the frying pan, you know.

"And you children.
I was a free ride for everybody, everywhere.
I was the first one up and the last one down
Seven days out of the week.
I always took the toast that got burned,

93

And the very smallest piece of pie.

I look at how some of your brothers treat their wives
    now,
And it makes me sick, 'cause it was me
That taught it to them. And they learned.
They learned that a woman doesn't
Even exist except to give.
Why, every single penny that I could save
Went for your clothes, or your books,
Even when it wasn't necessary.
Can't even remember once when I took
Myself downtown to buy something beautiful —
For me.

"Except last year when I got that red dress.
I found I had twenty dollars
That wasn't especially spoke for.
I was on my way to pay it extra on the washer.
But somehow — I came home with this big box.
Your father really gave it to me then.
'Where you going to wear a thing like that to —
Some opera or something?'
And he was right, I guess.
I've never, except in the store,
Put on that dress.

"Oh, Millie — I always thought if you take
Nothing for yourself in this world,
You'd have it all in the next somehow.
I don't believe that anymore.
I think the Lord wants us to have something —
Here — and now.

"And I'm telling you, Millie, if some miracle
Could get me off this bed, you could look
For a different mother, 'cause I would be one.
Oh, I passed up my turn so long
I would hardly know how to take it.
But I'd learn, Millie.
I would learn!"

It hung there in the closet
While she was dying, Mother's red dress,
Like a gash in the row
Of dark, old clothes
She had worn away her life in.

Her last words to me were these:
"Do me the honor, Millie,
Of not following in my footsteps.
Promise me that."

I promised.
She caught her breath,
Then Mother took her turn
In death.

Millie's mother was right; the Lord wants you to have something for yourself here and now. Yes, we were born to serve our fellowman, but what can be served on an empty platter; what can be learned from an empty book; what thirst can be quenched from an empty well?

There has to be some special time of the day or night or week (but never wait longer than a week) that belongs only to you; a time that you can spend frivolous WITHOUT FEELING GUILTY!

*Taken from *The Growing Season* by Carol Lynn Pearson, published by Bookcraft, Inc., copyright © 1976 by Bookcraft, Inc. Used with permission.

There was a young woman in my ward once who had NEVER left her four children. NEVER. She never came to an activity if she couldn't bring her children. She boasted of having never had a babysitter. Whether or not this young woman really did in her heart feel good about what she was doing NOW, what about LATER? She poured out all day and many nights, and never took time to replenish the supply, to fill the well. And in doing this, she was doing the children an injustice. Would they be able to make independent decisions later, when mother simply could not be there anymore? What of their self-esteem? What did they learn about from a mother who didn't take time to feed her spirit through private moments?

And after the children leave home, where will she be? What will she say to herself? What will she say to her companion after these years of 'separation'?

It is vital to take time to fill your wells after those who depend on you drain them dry. It is a wonderful birthright to be such a fountain or support to others. But in order to continue without running out, you must take time to refill, take time for only you.

7. *Persistence.* This requires self-discipline. Persistence is doing the job and making it look easy. Practice, practice, practice. President Heber J. Grant inspired all with his persistence to play baseball and his persistence to sing. He practiced and persisted until he made the job look easy!

Someone once said, "The coward never starts — the weak die on the way — only the strong come through."

Vince Lombardi, the great football coach, said, "The harder you fight for something, the harder it is to surrender." It becomes a part of you.

There is a wonderful story written by Blaine M. Yorgason called *Charlie's Monument* that tells a story of self-esteem and how persistence played an important role. Charlie was born crippled, twisted, and deformed. He was made fun of and not allowed at school. He struggled with tasks that most people found simple. When his parents died in his teen years, the town got together and gave him a job as "lookout" for Indians. Each day he had to climb a steep hill and there in solitude contemplate his worth, as he guarded the town. He decided to make a "monument" of rocks so that "they will always know that I have been here." (p. 45) It was an effort to build this monument; it took persistence. In the end, Charlie was the victor. His goals were realized because he never gave up. He persisted in his tasks until they became a part of him. He could never surrender to his physical deformities.

THE MONUMENT*

God,
Before He sent His children to earth
Gave each of them
A very carefully selected package
Of problems.

These,
He promised, smiling,
Are yours alone. No one
Else may have the blessings
These problems will bring you.

And only you
Have the special talents and abilities
That will be needed
To make these problems
Your servants.

Now go down to your birth
And to your forgetfulness. Know that
I love you beyond measure.

These problems that I give you
Are a symbol of that love.

The monument you make of your life
With the help of your problems
Will be a symbol of your
Love for me,
Your Father.

Blaine M. Yorgason

I counseled with a young woman who had been recently divorced. Her husband had left her alone with two small children. She felt useless, worthless, and a complete failure. All she could do was renumerate her weaknesses. As we talked about weaknesses and that they are really stepping stones rather than stumbling blocks, she seemed unconsolable. I explained to her that one of the reasons she felt such a lack of self-respect was because she wasn't even trying to conquer her weaknesses; she was letting them conquer her. When you indulge yourself (or give in to your weaknesses), YOU KNOW IT, and there is no self-respect.

She then said to me what I once felt, "Well. . .it seems a dreary existence to have to live in a continual battle against yourself. How can you ever find peace or happiness?"

Then I explained to her that happiness is not just attaining perfection, but rather, striving for it also. Most of us will never reach TOTAL perfection in mortality. The process of perfection will go on in the next life. If there wasn't a way to be happy in spite of our weaknesses, almost everyone would feel so despondent and suicidal. There is a way; the Lord has planned for that. As long as you are *striving* to *overcome*, your heart and mind will abound in feelings of self-control. These feelings lead to self-respect. Self-respect then creates within you happiness and peace.

President David O. McKay said: "There exists an eternal law that each human soul shall shape its own destiny." (*Gospel Ideals,* 1953, p. 300)

This eternal law, meaning God's law (See McConkie, *Mormon Doctrine,* "Eternal," p. 223), is what produces those natural inborn tendencies to overcome weaknesses and obstacles. It is through obedience to that law that happiness results. Whenever we disobey, we are unhappy. You can still be happy with yourself and not be satisfied or content with your levels of learning or achievement. As long as you are striving, the Lord blesses you with peace, the knowledge that He is pleased you are working.

You must develop the attitude that these are MY weaknesses, problems, and obstacles. These are MY strengths and attributes. They are for me alone. No one else can have them. Oh, I am so thankful for them! They will help me to master myself! I WILL master myself. I WILL press on with self-reliance and determination. Great works are performed, not by strength, but by persistence. With ordinary talent but extraordinary persistence, all things are attainable. Persistence gives power to weakness. I will begin my successes where other people's end in failure.

Chapter  Five

Handmaiden of the Lord

And out of small things proceedeth that which is great. Behold, the Lord requireth the heart and a willing mind...." (D & C 64:33-34)

Your small and fragile life which began in infancy has, through the years, developed into a noble womanhood in which your thoughts, feelings, and mind hold a sometimes thinly-veiled memory of the pre-existent life. What did you say to the Lord before you left? What covenants did you make with Him? What promises?

Have you stopped to wonder what the scene was like at His crucifixion? Have you pictured in your mind the hill, the crosses, the crowd, the bloody and bruised body? You were there. Those hosts in Heaven watched the entire scene, and you were there. As you watched Him hang and suffer and then finally "give up the ghost," what did you covenant at that moment?

Perhaps you said as the above scripture says, that even though you were small, one of billions of people, you would do your BEST, you would serve Him, you would seek to love others as He has loved you, you would give Him your heart and your willing mind.

Do you believe you said these things? Elder Bruce R. McConkie in his book, *Mormon Doctrine*, under the title section "Spirituality" says:

> All men do not come into this world with the same inclination toward or receptiveness of spiritual things. One of the greatest endowments a mortal man can receive is the gift of spirituality, the talent and ability to recognize and cleave unto the truth. 'My sheep hear my voice, and I know them, and they follow me,' our Lord said. (John 10:27) That is, his sheep so lived in pre-existence as to develop the gift of spirituality there; then coming to mortality, they brought that talent with them, and consequently they find it easy to believe and follow the true Shepherd. (*Mormon Doctrine*, p. 761)

Not all hear His voice. Those that do are members of His Church, and you are one of those. Because of your pre-existent life and valiancy, you came to earth with this *talent*, this *endowment*. (It is profound that he calls spirituality an endowment.) It is a gift predicated on your former life. With this gift comes the obligation to care for it, to strengthen it, and to realize that the possession of it enables you to be a Handmaiden of the Lord. You promised Him perfection, and perfection requires self-discipline.

Self-discipline is the ability to carry out a resolution after the enthusiasm is gone. How many projects, how many diets, how many exercise programs, how many more things have you been enthusiastic over, excited over, as you began, and then, as those projects became routine, you have lost interest?

"If it is to be, it is up to Me!"

No one but you can carry through with self-control and self-discipline. It is the second key, the second success factor (the first being the Holy Ghost) to any aspect of our happiness. In order to gain regulation of your thoughts and actions (in order to be obedient to all commandments and principles of the gospel), it is important that you:

1. Set priorities.
2. Establish goals.
3. Take action.

The following list suggests ways you may establish priorities and organize your thoughts. As you read through each one, write down the individual goals, short-term and long-term, that each one requires of you in order to establish your priority. This list is only suggestive and should be personalized as to individual requirements and aspirations.

MY RESOLUTIONS ESTABLISHING PRIORITIES
FOR GAINING SELF-CONTROL AND SELF-ESTEEM

I resolve to seek first the Kingdom of God and its righteousness with all my heart, might, mind, and strength and with an eye single to the glory of God;

I resolve that in order to be happy and enjoy peace of mind through self-respect and self-esteem, I must establish goals and accomplish them;

I resolve to be dependent upon the Holy Ghost for guidance and direction. I must live to deserve this inspiration, and I must obey when prompted by the Spirit.

I resolve that my first priority is to care for my mortal body which was created in the image of God and through which Godhood is possible through the atonement of Christ.

I resolve that my second priority is to be a companion to my husband; obey his counsel as he obeys the Lord.

I resolve that my third priority is to be a righteous mother in Zion.

I resolve that my fourth priority is to strengthen the family of my birth and the extended family members, and also the family of my husband.

I resolve that my fifth priority is to magnify my callings in His church.

I resolve that my sixth priority is to serve all mankind wherever I am able to serve.

I resolve that all priorities are interrelated and must be improved upon at the same time.

Here are a few suggestions to help you determine your own priorities:

"I resolve to seek first the Kingdom of God. . ."

1. Read scriptures daily.
2. Pray intently each day.
3. Fast once a month.
4. Allow the Holy Ghost to be my constant companion.
5. Develop faith.
6. Etcetera.

"I resolve in order to be happy and enjoy peace of mind through self-respect and self-esteem, I must establish goals and accomplish them;"

1. Work to perfect a talent.
2. Learn to play the piano.
3. Earn an extra $100 a month with my at-home business.
4. Develop my job at work into a greater challenge.
5. Take time to renew my strengths — time alone.
6. Finish college.
7. Learn to serve.
8. Etcetera.

"I resolve to be dependent upon the Holy Ghost. . ."

1. Pray for the Holy Ghost as a companion.
2. Obey the commandments.
3. Read all I can about the Holy Ghost and understand His role.

4. Listen for Him.
5. Obey His promptings.
6. Etcetera.

"I resolve my first priority is to care for my mortal body. . ."

1. Lose weight and maintain it.
2. Exercise regularly.
3. Be well groomed.
4. Get enough sleep, but not to excess.
5. Take time to relax.
6. Etcetera.

"I resolve my second priority is to be a good companion to my husband. . ."

1. Tell him every day that I love him.
2. Encourage him.
3. Support him in his callings.
4. Be his friend.
5. Etcetera.

"I resolve my third priority is to be a righteous mother. . ."

1. Take time with each child.
2. Teach them about the gospel.
3. Help Susie overcome her fear of public speaking.
4. Teach Johnny how to save for a mission.
6. Etcetera.

"I resolve my fourth priority is to serve my families. . ."

1. Prepare our genealogy.
2. Support them in their talents and lives.
3. Care for my ailing father.

4. Write to aging grandparents.
5. Teach the gospel to my non-member relatives.
6. Etcetera.

"I resolve my fifth priority is to magnify Church callings. . ."

1. Strive to read more.
2. Be better prepared.
3. Be 100 percent in visiting teaching.
4. Be a friend to my sisters I visit and not just go for the statistics.
5. Be dependable.

"I resolve my sixth priority is service to all mankind. . ."

1. Support the political candidate of my choice.
2. Volunteer for civic or community work.
3. Sponsor a refugee family.
4. Increase my welfare or fast offerings.
5. Visit the sick or needy.
6. Give all I can of myself, my time, and my money to the care and support of others.
7. Etcetera.

As you carefully study and contemplate each priority, think of the short-term and long-term goals involved. Ask yourself, "What would the Lord do here?" Be totally honest with yourself. And remember, you will never become anything you don't think about.

"As a man thinketh, so is he."

Now that you have thought about what you want to become, practice the "as if" principle. Act "as if" you are already there. If you want to smile more, then act "as if" you have the greatest smile in the world. If you want to be more successful, act "as if" you are successful.

Albert Einstein wrote, "The greatest tragedy in this life is what dies inside of man while he's still alive."

You are a God in embryo. Remember, you can do and be almost anything you want to do and be. It requires self-discipline and the desire to do it. A philosopher once wrote that desire is only thought and impulse. It is ephemoral and nebulous and of no value until it becomes its physical counterpart — action. This action is preparation. A lot of people have the DESIRE TO ACHIEVE. The difference between those who achieve and those who don't is that the achievers have the desire to PREPARE to achieve.

John Milton grasped the concept of man as God in embryo, even though he didn't understand it as such:

> The command of one's self is the greatest empire a man can aspire unto, and consequently, to be subject to our own passions is the most grievous slavery. He who best governs himself is best fitted to govern others.
>
> He who reigns within himself and rules his passions, desires and fears is more than a king.

Can you see that concept unfolding? How can you be a God, how can you govern others if you cannot govern yourself?

William Ernest Henley, in extreme physical pain and suffering, wrote this great masterpiece:

INVICTUS

Out of the night that covers me
Black as the Pit from pole to pole
I thank whatever Gods may be
For my unconquerable soul.

In the fell clutch of circumstance
I have not winced nor cried aloud.
Under the bludgeonings of chance
My head is bloody, but unbowed.

Beyond this place of wrath and tears
Looms but the Horror of the Shade,
And yet the menace of the years
Finds and shall find me unafraid.

It matters not how strait the gate,
How charged with punishments the scroll,
I am the master of my fate:
I am the captain of my soul.

Only a potential God could be the "captain of his soul." Success depends upon the backbone, not the wishbone. It was Henry Ford who said: "You can't build a reputation on what you are going to do."

And President David O. McKay said: "The rich rewards come only to the strenuous strugglers."

Expect perfection from yourself and those around you. Not expectations requiring harshness or anxiety, but expectations of love and accomplishment. You can become perfect in specific areas in your life, a talent, a gospel principle, a personality trait, etc. But, realize that you will not reach perfection in the TOTAL sense of the word in mortality. That TOTAL perfection is not necessary in order to inherit the celestial kingdom. Striving for it, working towards it, is the key. Total perfection is necessary to inherit the place of Godhood, however, it will take us into the eternities beyond mortality to reach that state. (See McConkie, *Mormon Doctrine,* "Perfection," p. 567.) The perfection of which I speak is perfection in *levels of learning* (gospel principles, talents, overcoming weaknesses, etc.). The standard must be set high enough so we can keep the eternal goal in perspective. You cannot be perfect in EVERYTHING you do. Priorities must be made and perfection achieved goal by goal. The Lord has asked us to be as perfect as He is for a reason. Let me illustrate.

When I decided to take flying lessons, I wanted the best

instructor there was. Rumors of instructors who "cranked" out students to pilots made me determined to find an excellent instructor. As I asked around for several months, one name kept coming up. After meeting the man and determining he was indeed a qualified instructor, I began my training. Difficult was not an adequate word for the course of instruction he put me through. If the FAA required you to fly within 300 feet of a target, he required you do it within 50 feet. If the FAA said have five hours under the instrument hood, he said ten. If the FAA required you to recover from a stall, he required recovery from a nose dive. He was demanding. The day of the check-ride came. Nervous does not even begin to describe my state of being that day! I could not sleep the night before; there were butterflies in my stomach, and my hands and nerves trembled. The written part went by too quickly, and the FAA examiner and I climbed into the airplane. I was amazed at how easy and simple the whole exam was; nothing compared to what my instructor had put me through. As the examiner was signing me off, he said, "If you could have a rating of perfect, I'd give it to you. Of all the students I have passed, your instructor's are the best. Nearly, if not perfect." After the noise and hilarity was over, and I had a quiet moment with this instructor, I told him what the examiner said. I asked, "Why do your students do so much better?" and he answered, "Because. . .I *expect* them to be perfect."

He learned the secret, and it paid off for him. If he'd expected anything less, that's exactly what the students would have given him — less. Had he been mediocre, as a lot of instructors are, his students would have been mediocre. When you are learning, you understand and know only the levels you are taught. If he had said the FAA requires you to fly 300 feet on this mark, his students would have done just that, perhaps not even realizing they could do better.

The Lord does nothing in mediocrity, and He EXPECTS you to be perfect. And he is the instructor and has set the levels of learning. "Be ye therefore perfect, even as your Father which is in heaven is perfect." (Matthew 5:48)

Any place along the way where you settle into complacency is mediocrity, and mediocrity is death to perfection. We tend to regard mediocrity as acceptable behavior. We do just enough to get by. Instead of taking one task to the point of absolute perfection, we just whitewash the fence instead of priming, sanding, and painting it. And do you realize what's happening by that example? Generations are being taught that mediocre is all that is expected.

Once my husband and I rated each other for fun. We were discussing our levels of achievement, mostly spiritual. We were rating each one in accordance with his or her potential. We decided that I was about 85 percent. Feeling fairly secure and smug about that, I was confident 85 percent was well within noteworthy acceptance. About an hour later, with — as Joseph Smith put it, pure intelligence flowing through me — came the thought and message that "85 percent is working Anita, but it's only the last 10-15 percent that counts to the Lord!"

It's that last ten percent that requires the most self-discipline in order to achieve perfection. In this life, we are only competing with ourselves.

This kind of competition, where supposedly no one is watching, is the hardest to achieve without the strictest of self-discipline — self-discipline to do *all* the Lord asks. Humbling yourself before Him and having faith in Him, only then can you unlock your own personal powers to self-discipline.

> And if men come unto me I will show unto them their weakness, I give unto men weakness that they may be humble; and my grace is sufficient for all men that humble themselves before me; for if they humble themselves before me, and have faith in me, *then will I make weak things become strong unto them.* (Ether 12:27)

The Lord shows you your weaknesses, and it is through an honest humility and effort that you can turn them into strengths.

How is that done? Suppose your weakness is impatience. You know it is your weakness. You feel so bad when you lose your temper. The Lord has revealed this weakness to you through feelings of remorse. Humbling yourself before Him, with a broken heart and contrite spirit, you repent. With faith in yourself and a positive mental attitude, you put your impatience foremost in your thoughts. As you put forth an earnest effort to control it, the control will come. With control comes strength, strength to be patient once, then twice, then several times, and finally, strength to overcome.

Why doesn't this happen more often in my life you say? I have tried but fallen back into my crevices of weakness.

It's because the self-discipline has not been there. I love President Kimball's now coined phrase "Lengthen Your Stride," but the best part of what he said has been left out: "I am not calling for flashy temporary differences in our performance levels, but a quiet resolve. . .to do a better job, to lengthen our stride. . ." (*Melchizedek Priesthood Personal Study Guide,* 1979-1980, p. 10)

Flashy, temporary differences in our performance levels is what I was referring to when I said that self-discipline is the ability to carry out a resolution after the enthusiasm is gone. Self-discipline is what President Kimball meant by "quiet resolve."

Resolve to make commitments and then commit to those resolutions. Lack of self-discipline grows on people; it starts with cobwebs and ends in iron chains.

Chapter  Six

Priesthood Partners

God created man in His image, we are taught. What does that mean? What is the image of God. "And I, God, created man in mine own image. . .male and female created I them." (Moses 2:27)

The image of God is a MAN AND A WOMAN. No, God is not both a man and a woman, there is another person, a partner, His wife. The image of God or Godhood is this partnership. "Neither is the man without the woman, neither the woman without the man. . ." (1 Corinthians 11:11)

President Kimball has elaborated on this scripture in a way that only a prophet can:

> And the scripture says, 'And I, God said unto mine Only Begotten, which was with me from the beginning: Let us make man [not a separate man, but a complete man, which is husband and wife] in our image, after our likeness; and it was so.' (Moses 2:26) What a beautiful partnership!
>
> Male and female created he *them*; and blessed *them*, and called *their* name Adam [Mr. and Mrs. Adam, I suppose, or Brother and Sister Adam] in the day when they were created. (Genesis 5:1-2) This is a partnership. (*Ensign*, March 1976, p. 71)

Elder Bruce R. McConkie has written: "An exalted and glorified Man of Holiness (Moses 6:57) could not be a Father unless a Woman of like glory, perfection, and holiness was associated with him as a Mother." (*Mormon Doctrine*, p. 516).

This means the Woman would hold equal standing and equal rights in the eyes of God. The Lord made woman from the rib of Adam. Now this was figurative, not literal. Eve was literally born as was Adam. Why then did the Lord see need to describe her as coming from Adams rib or side? The Prophet Joseph Smith enunciated a true observation of human nature:

> We have learned by sad experience that it is the nature and
> disposition of almost all men, as soon as they get a little authority,
> as they suppose, they will immediately begin to exercise
> unrighteous dominion. (D & C 121:39)

A figurative description was necessary to show she was not taken from his head to be higher nor from the feet to be lower but from the side to be equal. She was to be a helpmeet to him, and a helpmeet is not a servant.

In the beginning, in the Garden, Adam and Eve talked with God; He was their head. Each had direct communication with God. But with the Fall, this changed. God remained at the head, but the man stood between Him and the woman; man became the mediator between woman and her Father.

At first glance, this may make the woman appear inferior to the man. This is not true. Men and women are equal before God. The same laws, rules, and covenants apply to both equally. However, they are equal, but not the same. There is a very real difference between the sexes. In a song there is both melody and harmony — same song but different parts. The respective callings of each sex simply reflect the unique qualifications and temperments of each. The highest degree of Godhood is gained through the perfect blending of the qualities of man and woman. How could she be less than his equal? Is the harmony more important than the melody for the song to be perfect?

How we are regarded by others does influence our self-respect and our self-respect influences what we become. Held in low esteem, even contempt, some women exist in wastelands year after year, generation after generation. The condescension of the men in their lives is stoically endured — IT IS THEIR LOT, THEY BELIEVE. Because of the darkness of their lives, such women have lost all self-vision. And those men in their lives have likewise a horrible fate; they have lost all ability to see what has happened.

THE STEWARD

Heber looked at his lands
And he was pleased.
He'd be leaving them tomorrow, and his hands
Hurt with anticipated idleness.
But he knew there was no other way
When a man is seventy-eight and has to make
Two rest stops with a full bucket of milk
Between the barn and the kitchen.
Condominiums — do they have gardens? he
    wondered.
His son had arranged the place for them in town
And he was ready. He sat down
On the rock that knew his body
Better than the front room chair.

Could it really be fifty-five years ago
That sitting right there
They had talked?
His father's voice had never left him:
"Heber, I'm trusting to you
The most precious thing I've got.
I worked hard for this land. You know all about

The crickets and the Indians and the drought,
And the buckets of sweat it took
To make what you see today.
I'm giving it to you as a stewardship, son.
And when your time with the land is done
And we get together again
I'm going to call you to account.
I'm going to say, 'Heber, did you make it more
Than you found it? Did you watch it
And tend it? Did you make it grow?
Is it everything it can be?'
That's what I'll want to know."

Heber looked out on the fields
That for fifty-five years had been
Green and gold in proper turn —
On the fences and the barns and the ditches
And the trees in careful rows.
Even his father hadn't been able to get peaches.
He could hardly wait to report about those.

Margaret was finishing the last closet.
Just a few things were going to the city
And the rest rose in the mountain
On the back porch, waiting for the children
To sort through and take what they chose.
She opened the lid on a shoebox of valentines.
Perhaps just one or two for memory's sake?
But whose — whose would she take?

She put the box aside and reached again.
"What in the world?" In an instant her face
Cleared and in her hands was the old familiar
        case.

The violin. She hadn't touched it for forty years,
Hadn't thought of it for twenty at least.
Well, there they finally were — the tears.
Her mother's dishes hadn't done it,
Or the little Bible she had almost buried with
     Ellen,
Or the valentines —
But there they were for the violin.

She picked up the bow.
Had it always been so thin?
Perhaps her hand had grown so used to big
     things.
To kettles that weighed ten pounds empty,
And to milk cans and buckets of coal.
The wood felt smooth against her chin
As she put the bow to a string.
A slow, startled sound wavered, then fell.
How did she used to tune it? Ah, well,
No sense wasting time on moving day.
If Heber should come in, he would say,
"Well, there's Margaret — fiddlin' around
With her fiddle again."
He'd always said it with a smile, though.

"I could have done it," she said out loud.
"And it wouldn't have hurt him.
It wouldn't have hurt anybody!"

He hadn't minded that she'd practiced two hours
Every afternoon — after all, she got up at five
And nobody in the world could criticize
The way she kept the house
Or the care she gave to the children.

And he was proud that she was asked
To play twice a year at the church.
And music made her so happy.
If she missed a day things were not quite
So bright around the house.
Even Heber noticed that.

And then she was invited to join the symphony in
    town.
Oh, to play with a real orchestra again!
In a hall with a real audience again!

"But, Margaret, isn't that too much to ask
Of a woman with children and a farm to tend?"
"Oh, Heber, I'll get up at four if I have to
I won't let down — not a bit. I promise!"

"But I couldn't drive you in,
Not two nights a week all year round,
And more when they're performing."

"I can drive, Heber. It's only twenty miles.
I'd be fine. You would have to be
With the children, though, until Ellen
Is a little older."

"But I couldn't guarantee two nights a week —
Not with my responsibilities to the farm,
And to the Church."

"Heber, there's no way to tell you
How important this is to me. Please, Heber.
I'll get up at four if I have to."

But Heber said no.
What if something happened to the car?
And then it just wouldn't look right
For a man's wife to be out chasing
Around like that. What would it lead to next?
Once in a while he read of some woman
Who went so far with her fancy notions
That she up and left her family, children and all.
He couldn't see Margaret ever doing that,
But it's best to play it safe.
Two nights a week — that was asking a lot.

So Heber said no.
It was his responsibility to take care of her.
She had been given to him, in fact.
He remembered the ceremony well,
The pledges, the rings.
And he didn't take it lightly.
She had been given to him,
And it was up to him to decide these things.
So Heber said no.

She had seemed to take it all right,
Though she was quieter than usual
And more and more an afternoon would pass
Without her practicing.

He didn't really notice how it happened —
The shrinking of her borders,
The drying up of her green.
If Heber ever thought about it in later years
He marked it up to the twins.
Motherhood was hard on a woman,
And Margaret just wasn't quite the same as

117

before.

She laid the violin in its case
And rubbed away the small wet drop
On her thin hand.

"I could have done it," she said aloud.
"Heber, you didn't understand.
I could have done it and not hurt anybody.
I would have gotten up at four!"

Slowly she made her way to the porch
And put the violin with the things
For the children to sort through.
"Will any of them remember?
I don't think so."

Heber gave a last look at his lands
And he was pleased.
He could face his father with a clear mind.
"Here's my stewardship," he would say,
"And I think you'll find
I did everything you asked.
I took what you gave me — and I made it more."

He got up and started toward the house,
Putting to his lips
A long, thin piece of hay.
"Better get movin'. Margaret will be
Needing me for supper right away."

Carol Lynn Pearson

Taken from *The Growing Season* by Carol Lynn Pearson, published by Bookcraft, Inc. Copyright © 1976 by Bookcraft, Inc. Used by permission.

Women as a general rule throughout history have never been shown the respect, protection, guidance, or love they both needed and deserved. They are the impoverished sex. However, a real battle ensues. Many modern women are striking back but in a damaging and bitter way. If the role of woman is to be preserved, and yet her self-esteem and desires fulfilled, she must understand what her true cause is and what God has intended for her from the beginning and why He said, "thy desire shall be to thy husband, and he shall rule over thee." (Moses 4:22)

There is an order in Heaven, and this order comes through the patriarchal order. Under the patriarchal order of marriage, the patriarch as father or husband, holds the keys of Priesthood for his family. The Priesthood makes a man an officer in the Kingdom of God. Likewise, a woman commits herself to the law or guidance of the Priesthood. It is the Lord's unbroken chain of stewards. These stewardships extend back into the eternities. Just as no one can come back to the Father except through Christ, no one can come back to Christ except through the Melchezidek Priesthood. When a woman honors the Priesthood, she is honoring her Father in Heaven and preparing to come back into His presence. It is the Lord's way and law of order.

Brigham Young said:

> I do not know what the Lord could have put upon women worse than he did upon Mother Eve, where he told her: 'Thy desire shall be to thy husband.' Continually wanting the husband. . .I do not know that the Lord could have put upon women anything worse than this. I do not blame them for having these feelings. . . .says a woman of faith and knowledge, 'I will make the best of it; it is a law that man shall rule over me, . . .' and by doing so she has promises that others do not have. (Journal of Discourses 16:167)

The obligation to submit to the rule (leadership) of a "fallen" man (Adam) after having enjoyed the personal guidance of God is descension for the woman. It was part of the "curse" for the Fall in the garden. Yet by her keeping this commandment she will find the means of her exaltation. By enduring to the end, a woman with perfect understanding will share equally eternal life with her companion. All debts will be fully paid — a woman's debt to the Priesthood for its efforts in her behalf, and the Priesthood's debt to woman for her indispensable part in its eternal labor.

> And then the Priesthood will wish to proclaim their debt to these their helpmeets without whom the Priesthood could not have worked out their destiny. And the Priesthood shall bow in reverence and love unbounded before these mothers who did the service the Priesthood could not do, and thank and praise them for bearing their children... (J. Reuben Clark, RSM 33:804)

Because women are under the direction of the Priesthood gives no man the right to assume unrighteous dominion, and certainly no woman can or should follow a man to hell.

A beautiful woman whose husband recently left her for a younger woman after 35 years of marriage lamented to me: "I did everything for him, even to the point of becoming inactive in the Church because he wanted me to." Now she has found herself with nothing, not even the relationship with the Father that she needs more than ever at this time.

Because we as women receive "direction" by the Priesthood does not mean our opinions or decisions are of no value if questioned by the Priesthood. Often I have seen a woman, confident in a certain opinion or decision she has formed become mentally disheveled because she heard some in "authority" give a different point of view. Everyone is entitled to his or her own opinion and the right to make personal decisions.

When it comes to the principles and ordinances of the gospel, the directives for the Church come from the Prophet. Strict attention, heed, and obedience is to be given the Prophet's counsel. But each man AND WOMAN is entitled to his or her own personal revelation as to what is best for each of them. Don't ever doubt those ideas, opinions, or promptings that have been confirmed by the Spirit to you. Someone else's opinion may be of value for them. And then again, you will learn a great deal from others' thoughts. But be confident in your own.

The Priesthood is the greatest power on earth, and you can benefit through that power, whether it is in your home or not. Wife, mother, sister in the gospel, young woman, these are all priesthood callings.

While most women of the Church today can call readily upon the authority of the Priesthood, our pioneer sisters were often left to manage for themselves while the men were away on missions for months and years. They had to call upon the gifts of the Spirit, especially healing, to care for their families and themselves.

But I believe there has never been a time when the women (and girls) of the Church need the aid of the Holy Ghost more than today and in the days ahead. These are perilous last days. The future holds dangerous and testing trials. It is not unreasonable to contemplate that many women of the Church will yet be called upon to carry burdens usually borne by husbands and fathers. (Journal of Discourses 3:15) It is wise for each woman in the church to seek after her own "Priesthood" potential and spiritual gifts — to develop her strength as a partner with God.

Joseph Smith said in speaking to the women at the time he organized the Relief Society: "The keys of the Kingdom are about to be given to them that they may be able to detect anything false, as well as to the elders." (Nauvoo R.S. minutes 17 March 1842)

He also said: "If you live in accord with your privileges, angels cannot be restrained from being your associates." (Women's Exponent, 14 March 1913)

Right now many of you carry burdens usually borne by husbands and fathers. Some of you are divorced, some single (never married), some widowed, or with a non-member or inactive husband (or father). Some of you are married to active men who hold Church positions that take them out of or away from the home often. "If you live in accord with your privileges, angels cannot be restrained from being your associates." What a tremendous *Priesthood* protection and strength!

Divorced or single women have a great test of faith. They often feel more sensitive to failure because the Church is so family oriented and so are the Church members as a main body. Well-meaning members say, "You'll be okay; don't feel bad about being single." But then they ignore those special needs.

I still remember those feelings I had right after I divorced my first husband. It was, at that point though, that I began on the way to a healthier self-esteem. It was those reborn feelings of self-worth which caused me to get up and initiate changes in my life. However, as I sat in Church with my children, I felt half of a whole. I felt a totally vapid area in my life. I didn't tell anyone; no one really knew for weeks.

Then a loving sister that I hardly knew came up to me one Sunday and explained she'd found out about the divorce because she was in charge of the softball program. When she called my ex-husband, he had told her. Then she did something so simple which changed my feelings of emptiness from that moment forward. She handed me an *Ensign* and said, "I got this from the library for you. There's an article by a divorced woman in here; I thought you'd like to read it. Maybe you'll enjoy hearing some of the things you've been thinking."

I read the article. It wasn't anything that gave me extra strength. Strength wasn't what I needed. I had already crossed over to a better self-image and that had helped me make a decision to divorce. But what I needed was to know that I was accepted. I wasn't really HALF OF A WHOLE. I was a whole; I was worth something all on my own. The article didn't do that; sweet La

Donna Davis did that for me. She took the time to let me know I was okay, and it was okay with her.

And single women in the Church are a WHOLE. No matter why you are single, if you love the Lord and could have a celestial marriage if you had the opportunity, the Lord will see to it that one day you do. (Joseph Fielding Smith, *Doctrines of Salvation*, 2:76) Nothing will be withheld from the faithful.

> Single women's lives are just as important as non-single women's lives. . .One way to get away from the self-pity of feeling deprived is to understand that sex roles have been vastly overdone. Brigham Young tried to expand men's and women's minds in this matter. 'The ladies can learn to keep books as well as the men; we have some few, already, who are just as good accountants as many of our brethren. Why not teach more to keep books and sell goods, and let them do this business.' . . . 'We believe that women are useful, not only to sweep houses, wash dishes, make beds, and raise babies, but they should stand behind the counter, study law or physic. . .to enlarge their sphere of usefulness for the benefit of society at large. In following these things they but answer the design of their creation' (Oscar W. McConkie, *She Shall Be Called Woman*, pp. 113-114)

There is much a single woman can do to enlarge her sphere of usefulness to the world and herself. And in doing so, she can exercise her own "Priesthood" callings and gifts. Harold B. Lee said:

> Those without mates — in your ranks are some of the noblest members of the church — faithful, valiant, striving to live the Lord's commandments, to help build the kingdom on earth, and to serve your fellowmen.
>
> Life holds so much for you. Take strength in meeting your challenges. There are so many ways to find fulfillment, in serving those who are dear to you, in doing well the tasks that are before you in your employment or in your home. The Church offers so much opportunity for you — to help souls, beginning with your own, to find the joy of eternal life. (*Strengthening the Home*, pamphlet, 1973, p. 8)

The Priesthood is the greatest power on earth, and we can benefit through that power by:

1. Realizing it has been given to man as a Divine order of authority from God — a stewardship.

2. It's power is available to any woman, whether the priesthood is in her home or not.

3. Our callings from the Lord are priesthood callings.

4. By submitting to the priesthood, in righteousness, we are participating in our part of the plan of salvation.

5. We have the power to call upon spiritual (priesthood) gifts for our personal use and for the benefit of our families.

6. The male cannot gain salvation without the female.

7. Our priesthood partners cannot grow or develop to full potential unless enhanced by female spirituality and support.

Some inborn characteristics and qualities are uniquely feminine. God designed it that way. There were no mistakes in Heaven. Women have a definite responsibility to not only retain those specific feminine characteristics and qualities, but to add to them — to leave this world having made their personal environment better than what they had found it!

Chapter  Seven

Be A Blessing To All Those With Whom You Associate

President Joseph F. Smith once said:

I think it is very important that. . .women should early form some design, some definite purpose in life. Let that resolve be a noble one, a good one; something with a view of benefitting others as well as one's self. Perhaps your sphere may be in the household. If so, let every member feel that you are indispensable to the comfort of the home, by your good works and your love and patience. . .

Be in a certain degree independent; to the degree of usefulness, helpfulness and self-reliance, though no human beings can be said truly to be independent of their fellow beings and there is no one reckless enough to deny our utter dependence on our Heavenly Father. Seek to be educated in the highest meaning of the term; get the most possible service out of your time, your body and brain, and let all your efforts be directed into honorable channels, that no effort shall be wasted, and no labor result in loss or evil.

Seek the very best society; be kind, polite, agreeable, seeking to learn whatever is good, and comprehend the duties of life *that you may be a blessing to all those with whom you associate,* making the very most and best of your lot in life. . .

> There are people fond of saying that women are the weaker vessels. I don't believe it. Physically, they may be; but spiritually, morally, religiously, and in faith, what man can match a woman who is really convinced? (*Gospel Doctrine*, 7th edition, p. 352)

Understand how great you are in the creation of all things. God made you just "a little lower than the angels." You have a great work to do, one that no other can do, as the primary song says.

Rose Kennedy, the mother of President John Kennedy, said once that she was convinced that she had special work on earth which God had given her to do here, and if she didn't do it, it just simply wouldn't ever get done. That is all truth. You have a work that no other can do.

We talk in the Church always about how much we need the Lord, but realize that He needs us, too. His kingdom cannot go forth without obedient, loving, worshipping servants. And we always tell Him "thank you," but have you stopped and realized that there are many times He says "thank you." These are the moments which fill your soul to the brim, bring you such joy, such a wonderful feeling of self-worth. "A glorious Being knows I am here, has seen what I've done, and has said thank you!"

Whether those thank you's are in the form of a blessing, an answer, an opportunity, or a warm feeling in your heart, it is real, and if you listen, you can hear clearly, "Well done, thou good and faithful servant."

Recently my father gave me a blessing. Usually, my husband does this, but every now and then I ask for a father's blessing. As he laid his hands upon my head, I felt a sweet spirit encircle me through the power of the priesthood. In a very special way I received a "thank you" for the good that I had done thus far in my life. What a sweet joy I felt and great warmth. He knows where I am, even here in Las Vegas.

Antigonus was an eminent field general for Alexander the Great. Upon the eve of a great battle with an enemy, after much preparation and planning, it was discovered the army of Antigonus was greatly outnumbered. Morning came and out went the battle cry, but Antigonus' men did not attack, so great was their fear. They were about to retreat when Antigonus arrived and asked what was wrong with his men. The captain told him they were afraid because they were so outnumbered. Antigonus looked directly at him, thought for a moment and asked, "How many do you count me for?" This undeflatable attitude quickly spread through the camps, and the enemy lost the battle to Antigonus.

The Lord needs you. How many does He count you for? Are you a mighty army? Are you a blessing to all those with whom you associate?

President Kimball said:

> I hope that if any of God's children are out in spiritual darkness, you will come to them with a lamp and light their way; if they are out in the cold of spiritual bleakness with its frigidity penetrating their bones, you will come to them holding their hands a little way, you will walk miles and miles with them lifting them, strengthening them, encouraging them and inspiring them. (Featherstone, *Charity Never Faileth,* p. 56)

This book has talked about your "needs." It has laid out a plan by which those "needs" can be turned into "tools." Tools such as inner strength, calmness, charity, patience, virtue, confidence, self-discipline that can be used for furthering the Lord's Kingdom on the earth. Remember, you can control no one but yourself. But with that control, you can influence the world.

Your families, husbands, and children need you; the Lord needs you; I need you.

My greatest hope in this book is that you can read it with the spirit in which it was written, that you can "feel" through the pages the love I have for you. That it is no VAIN REPETITION. Spending the hours and time in preparing this work for YOU, I have grown to love you *individually,* and just every now and then, get a glimpse of that overwhelming love the Savior has for all.

I have written this book because I am a woman and have felt all the frustrations, thoughts, guilts, and fears that you have felt. This book took 34 years to write. I've wanted to share it with you because it doesn't matter how old you are, all that this book contains will work — if you will commit to it.

There was a stake meeting recently in which two men were overheard saying that it was good to come there and get all fired up "even though they'd just go home and not do anything about it."

I hope you will not read this book and then say, "Oh, that was a nice book to read, I really should do something," and then put the book down and never do anything. You will have wasted your money and time. I hope (and pray) you will ACT. As President Kimball says, "DO IT!" Not tomorrow, or in the morning, but RIGHT NOW.

Understand that the purpose in accumulating knowledge is tenuous and flacid unless you put it to use. If you have "read everything" and are a "do nothing," you have moved closer towards atrophy and guilt feelings. Self-esteem can never develop. It is better to be fired up and fail than to be fired up and never try. Failure can be overcome. Fear of failure is death to growth.

The Lord is not preparing candidates for the terrestrial or telestial worlds, only celestial candidates. The Lord is calling for the winners. A lot of people have the WILL to win. The difference between losers and winners is that the winners had the WILL TO PREPARE TO WIN.

This is a book dealing with preparation. I promise you, if you will take these things, these principles and ideas, and apply them in your personal life, and you ACT and PERSIST, your life will never be the same again.

You will taste success and once you do, you'll never be satisfied with less. I promise you that you will find joy, love of life, love of family and people, love of the Lord, and life to your whole being! You will have a warmth and inner peace that will constantly strengthen you.

I want you to write to me (my address is on the last page of this book), and pour out your thoughts and successes and failures. Let me be your friend if you need a place to "return and report." Send them anonymously if you want. We all have something to learn from each other.

If it is possible to help a woman to moral regeneration and renewed self-vision, the first step must be to redeem her self-esteem. The gospel of Jesus Christ does that for us in a way that only the truth can.

Who are you? . . . A daughter of God. What can you know? . . . All that God knows. What manner of woman should you be? . . . As the Master is. What can you hope for? Peace in this world, of mind and spirit, and crowns of glory and exaltation in the world to come.

Sisters, with such knowledge as this, depression and lack of identity should never survive. There is no road to success but through a clear and strong purpose. Nothing can take its place. A garden is just plain ground until it's planted. Each woman is her own gardener. In the furrows of her mind are seeds that bring forth a royal harvest. May you be a blessing to all those with whom you associate.

LIFE PLAN FOR GAINING SELF-ESTEEM
AND KEEPING IT

I.   Identify yourself.

     A.   You are a daughter of God

         1.   Be honest with yourself.
         2.   Describe your qualities and weaknesses.
         3.   Realize you are a God in embryo; what can you do to develop that embryo?

     B.   You lived with Him before you came here.

         1.   What were you instructed in pre-earth life?
         2.   What were you taught and what are your talents?
         3.   You loved the Lord and His plan.
         4.   Pay the price for excellence.
         5.   Continue pre-existent training here on earth and learn from others.

     C.   God loves you dearly.

         1.   Everyone is discouraged, even great prophets.
         2.   Discouragement is from Satan, not the Lord.
         3.   God asks you to be perfect and then gives you weaknesses by which to perfect yourself.
         4.   Positive mental attitude is a power over Satan. The Lord has given us the ability to control our thoughts.

D. It is possible to become like God.

    1. List your qualities, your weaknesses, and compare with God's.
    2. Record thoughts, goals, and progress in a journal.
    3. Return and report to yourself.

II. Develop your identity.

  A. Spiritually.

    1. Strive for the personality of Jesus Christ.
    2. Develop your own relationship with the Lord; depend on no one else.
    3. This can be accomplished through:
      a. Prayer — seek to pray more sincerely and intently.
      b. Holy Ghost — read and learn about the Holy Ghost and his role. Understand He has a critical role in helping you toward Godhood. Learn to live by the Spirit.
      c. Read scriptures daily — let them go through your being.
      d. Live righteously — obey all the commandments, repent often, and be humble.
      e. Develop charity — the pure love of Christ — live your life to serve others. Be forgiving.

  B. Physically.

    1. Proper Diet — make a commitment for the rest of your life.
    2. Good Exercise Plan — be consistent and realistic.

3. Proper Clothing — dress attractively. Learn about clothing, fit, styles, and what looks good on your body.
4. Cleanliness.
5. Makeup and Hair.

C. Socially.

1. Gain self-confidence — competence creates self-confidence.
   a. Learn to do one thing to perfection before taking on something else.
   b. Compete only with yourself.
   c. Be honest with yourself, about your feelings.
   d. Assume responsibility for your decisions.

2. Learn to handle rejection.
   a. Don't take it personally.
   b. Learn that the MOLD is not a correct path.
   c. Single, divorced, or childless sisters have as much purpose in life as any other woman.

3. Organize yourself.
   a. The only way you can manage your time is to have a plan for it.
   b. Let a schedule serve you; do not serve it.

4. Continue to increase your knowledge.
   a. Seek and learn out of the best books.
   b. Learn how to be a good conversationalist and enjoy people.
   c. Develop your talents (list them and plan to increase them).

     5. Take time for yourself — fill the well.

     6. Persist and ACT — keep self-discipline out in front.

III.   Strive for self-discipline.

    A. Set priorities (see list Chapter III).
    B. Establish goals — record in journal.
    C. Take action.
    D. Expect perfection from yourself.

IV.   Benefit through the priesthood.

    A. The Lord placed man and woman here equally.
    B. The separate roles are necessary for exaltation of the family.
    C. The Priesthood gives no man a right to unrighteous dominion.
    D. The Lord needs strong women in these last days.
    E. Learn to benefit through Priesthood callings, blessings, and its power.
    F. Single women are an equal part of the Priesthood Plan.

V.   Be a blessing to all those with whom you associate.

    A. The Lord needs you.
       1. He appreciates your helping him to carry out His work.
       2. Make sure He can count on you.
       3. Be a beacon light to all those who need you.

    B. Concentrate your efforts on self-esteem.

1. Make commitments for the rest of your life.
2. PREPARE yourself to win.

C. Carry the gospel to all the earth.

D. Share what you learn.

"People don't plan to fail — they just fail to plan."

Books In Print

Self-Esteem and the Physical You
Self-Esteem and the Social You
Power To Be You (Tape)
The Young Woman and Her Self-Esteem

If *you* have any comments concerning this book and how it has helped you or your personal feelings about self-esteem or to learn more about the "Women's Enrichment" Seminars being conducted, write to:

ANITA CANFIELD
5895 WEST PATRICK LANE
LAS VEGAS, NEVADA 89118